HOW
TEENAGERS
THINK

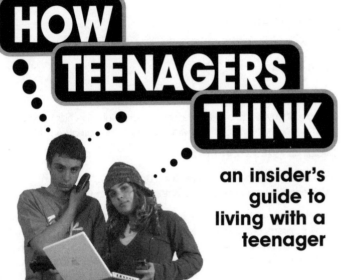

an insider's
guide to
living with a
teenager

Editor: Roni Jay

jellyellie

new tricks for old dogs

Published by White Ladder Press Ltd
Great Ambrook, Near Ipplepen, Devon TQ12 5UL
01803 813343
www.whiteladderpress.com

First published in Great Britain in 2007

10 9 8 7 6 5 4 3

© jellyellie 2007

The right of jellyellie to be identified as author of this work has been asserted by
her in accordance with the Copyright, Designs and Patents Act 1988.

13-digit isbn 978 1 905410 13 2

British Library Cataloguing in Publication Data
A CIP record for this book can be obtained from the British Library.

Designed and typeset by Julie Martin Ltd
Cover design by Julie Martin Ltd
Cover photograph Jonathon Bosley

Printed and bound by TJ International Ltd, Padstow, Cornwall
Cover printed by St Austell Printing Company
Printed on totally chlorine-free paper
The paper used for the text pages of this book is FSC certified.
FSC (The Forest Stewardship Council) is an international
network to promote responsible management of the world's forests.

FSC
Mixed Sources
Product group from well-managed
forests and other controlled sources

Cert no. SGS-COC-2482
www.fsc.org
© 1996 Forest Stewardship Council

White Ladder books are distributed in the UK by Virgin Books

White Ladder Press
Great Ambrook, Near Ipplepen, Devon TQ12 5UL
01803 813343
www.whiteladderpress.com

Contents

Dedication

Choosing a dedication has been the trickiest thing about writing this book, but I would like to dedicate it to Pappy; thank you for passing me your entrepreneurial flair and writing talents. I promise I won't run away with the ball – not now I can (hopefully) afford to buy lots and lots and lots of them.

Preface

Thank you for picking up *How Teenagers Think*, I hope you will learn a lot from it, please check out my website, blah blah blah – yaaaawn!

Instead of boring blabber, I thought you might be interested to know why I have a preface and introduction, because it always bemuses me when books have a foreword, preface, overview, introduction, and 100 other things that surely cover the same thing.

The reason I have two of these is because I originally wanted to write a few paragraphs giving you some general background information about myself, my family, and my life in general. I wanted to call it 'About Me', but dad commented that it might be a little egotistical – and I suppose I agree. So I have cheated and written much the same thing, but under the disguise as a preface.

Let me begin:

In case you hadn't noticed, my name is jellyellie, and I've done the most un-teenager-like thing of writing a book. I know, I think it's a little weird sometimes too. At the time of writing this book, I am 15.

For the past few years I have been home educated. I went to school until I was 14 but the whole education system became too stifling. I spent a good few months feeling extremely frustrated with the way I was being held back in so many areas until my parents decided to pull me out of school, and I have thrived ever since.

I live in Surrey, with my parents and my brother. My mum is

undoubtedly the most kind and caring person in the world, and does far too much to help other people. My brother, Alex, is currently 14 – that's him with me on the front cover. He's dead cool, except he's not interested in anything unless it has four wheels and an engine; yup, a petrolhead like my dad. Ah, my dad – he's amazing. Basically he acts as my agent and manager, but gets nothing for his troubles except having to make excuses to his boss for why he's been late for meetings – of course he doesn't tell them it was because he was accompanying me to a meeting in London or something. Not that I have a big ego… well, you can make up your mind about that after reading this book, but it's no secret that I have my opinions and I like to make sure everyone hears them.

If you are a Myers-Briggs fan like myself, you may be interested to know that I am an ENTP. So if there are any handsome, dark haired INFJs out there, I'd love to hear from you.

In fact, I would love to hear from you anyway – I love meeting new people, hearing new ideas, and just generally having fun. So please feel free to email me at **jellyellie@HowTeenagersThink.com** with any comments, criticisms, or crazy Dr Pepper recipes. Ahh yes… I sort of have this thing about Dr Pepper. I kind of like it. A lot.

I suppose I ought to mention my love for money and all-things-entrepreneurial. As you will go on to read, my main goal in life is to run my own multi-billion pound company, be stinking rich, and live on a yacht travelling round the Mediterranean. I recently discovered what 'magnanimous philanthropist' means, and I'd love to be able to put it on my business card one day.

I must also put in a quick plug for my websites **www.ellie-g.co.uk** and **www.bluejackQ.com** (and **www.HowTeenagersThink.com**, of course). ellie-g.co.uk is my personal website which I have updated since I was 11, and contains lots of funny stories, weird Dr Pepper stuff, photos, info on my hobbies, and other crazy things. bluejackQ is a bit different; it's a website I started when I was 13, and is about 'bluejacking' – the art of using Bluetooth enabled mobile phones to anonymously send messages to other Bluetooth mobiles. I started it as a small hobby site when I couldn't find any other websites about bluejacking, but the media seemed to like it a bit too much and it has grown to be the world's most cited website on the subject.

Finally, perhaps I should be a bit conventional and thank a few people, as without their generous help and support this book would never exist. I would like to thank Roni for being the most fab publisher anyone could ever wish for, and Rich for filling me with inspiration and motivation – I hope you like it. I would also like to thank everybody else at White Ladder Press who has helped with this book in some way; you truly are an amazing team.

I would also like to thank each and every one of my friends. For those of you who contributed a comment or interview – and you know who you are, even if your name has been changed to protect your innocence – I can't begin to thank you enough; without your help this book wouldn't be what it is. I'd also like to raise a can of Dr Pepper to everybody else I know, as you have all helped in some way whether you realise it or not.

Before you set off on your journey through *How Teenagers Think*, I will answer a question I have already been asked many times, and I'm sure will be asked many more times in the future – if only people actually read these damn things…

Why did I decide to write this book? Well, it all started when I had an argument with my mum in a bookshop...

1

Introduction

I'm not having such a good day today. I spent the morning in town with my mum and brother Alex, and as Alex put it, "Why do you have to comment on everything mum says?". It's true: everything mum said, I questioned. Parents, does that sound familiar? You're nodding. I thought so.

We went into a bookshop to buy a book for my grandad's birthday. Alex spotted a juicy war book, and mum thought it was a good choice. Mum could see that I had my eye on the new Andy McNab book, so added that to our basket as well. Both of the books we had picked were '3 for 2', so we needed another book. This is always the hardest part, picking the damn freebie.

I suggested that Alex should pick a book he liked the look of because he doesn't read enough, but he really didn't want one. It's frustrating that Allie doesn't read books – he's missing out on so much. You can learn so much from reading, and it's the only way your writing will *truly* develop. As technology has barged its way into our lives, reading is a pastime that is becoming more and more uncommon and geeky amongst teenagers.

On the other hand, those teen fiction books that talk about sex and romance seem to be doing quite well. However, they're totally uninspiring, lack any real plot or character depth, and are just not real books at all.

One of the best – no, *the* best – book I've read is *Battle Cry* by Leon Uris. It's about new recruits to the Marines in the Second World War and is a fantastically emotional, engaging book. The 700 pages which once overwhelmed me soon became 400 pages, 300, 200… oh, have I finished? Is there a sequel? Are they still alive today? Whoops – it's just fiction.

I'd never read a 'war book' before, and was never intending to. I like crime books, non-fiction mainly, but novels are fun too. I've also become very interested in psychology, so I quite enjoy reading popular psychology books and, forgive me for my geekiness, psychology textbooks. Ahem.

Anyway, you get the picture: war books are definitely not my thing.

So how did I end up reading *Battle Cry*?

Simple answer: Dad bought it for me.

Extended answer: I was going on holiday with a friend – more on this later – and was planning to just take two true crime books with me. At this point dad had already bought me *Battle Cry*; he had given it to me as a surprise present one day, but at the time I think I really would have preferred another drug smuggling one.

Just as I was about to shut my suitcase to go on holiday, dad asked me if I'd packed *Battle Cry*. I hadn't, so dad put it in my case. I wasn't really that keen for him to do so; it wasn't that I was reluctant, I just though it wouldn't be a great holiday read… bit depressing and all that… well, OK, I wasn't really looking forward to reading an old war book. Much more fun learning how Howard Marks smuggled the ole' beneficial herbs around the world.

In the end, I ended up finishing my two drug smuggling books within about five days anyway, so I had no choice but to read *Battle Cry*.

Battle Cry. What an amazing book. I won't go into a rant (rants are dad's territory) about how awesome it is, but here's an example:

I'm one of those people who doesn't have a favourite film, a favourite author, a favourite band; heck I don't even have a favourite music genre. I like too much stuff – including books. But for the very first time ever, the second I read the last word in *Battle Cry*, I knew I had turned a point in my life. I had a favourite, a favourite book. *Battle Cry*, I love you. Dad, thank you.

◎

So what was the point in you reading all of that? What did you, as a person, a parent, gain from it? Well, I'm not sure really. I just sort of got onto the subject of books because we were talking about the bookshop, and I thought the *Battle Cry* bit fitted in quite nicely, so I carried on with it and saw where we ended up. Well here's where we have ended up, and actually, I now know what you've gained from reading it: an introduction, a little insight into me, my personality, and a little about my dad. You may think you didn't learn much, but your unconscious mind got a lot more out of it than you think.

And it's at this point you start to worry that the whole of this book will be a load of garble and I can flog it to you by saying "You may think you didn't learn much, but your unconscious mind got a lot more out of it than you think." Don't worry, that's not the case at all.

My aim in writing this book is to give you an insight into how we teenagers think. I reckon the emphasis on understanding teenagers has been totally lost over recent years. With so much parenting advice from middle-aged psychologists whose teenage years are long forgotten, people have missed a valuable source of information staring them right in the face.

To research Roman architecture, you examine the remains. To solve a crime, you interrogate suspects. To learn about bringing up teenagers… surely, you ask teenagers for their thoughts. What a brilliant idea! Maybe I should write a book?

As well as drawing on my own experiences as a teenager, there will be lots of interviews with a wide range of my friends scattered throughout the book. With over 200 online contacts on my MSN list from countries all over the world – England, Ireland, France, Belgium, Italy, Germany, Holland, Brazil, Australia, America, and Canada to name a few – I have a truly global pool of teenagers to interview.

With regard to the type of teenager I'm assuming you have, the majority of stuff will work with 'normal' teenagers – those who perhaps do OK at school, obey you 10% of the time, never help around the house, request double the pocket money you'd like to give them, have a boyfriend four years older than them, etc. I don't like sweeping statements like 'normal teenagers', but sometimes it has to be done.

So you think your teen is a bit more off the rails than that? Ah don't worry. They're just seeing how far they can push you. Well, maybe you should worry – but then you'd be using all of your mental power concentrating on bad thoughts, when you could just as easily be thinking positively about ways of helping your teen. And that's where this book comes in.

Read it from front to back, take snippets from here and there – whatever works for you. I'd also be willing to bet you £5 (cheques payable to jellyellie, thankyouplease) that your teen will want to read this book too – and that's fantastic.

Now, I know most people die when they hear the phrase 'it's a good idea to take notes', but I'm actually trying it for the first time ever whilst reading some psychology books and it's amazing how much more you feel you learn. So, why not give it a go? You don't have to write an essay on each chapter, just a sentence here and there. Mind maps are great ideas too. In fact, I've even been so kind as to…

> …give you these little key notes along the way, to sum up a point I'm making…

…which often come together at the end of the chapter as pieces of practical 'homework' for you to go away and do. So if nothing else, jot down some of the key points, and do the homework – it's there solely for one purpose: to help you build a great relationship with your teens.

Now then, shall we get back to the bookshop? Ready to let your unconscious mind learn a little more? Let's go!

◎

So we're still in the bookshop hunting for this third freebie book. At the moment we have a war book for my grandad and an Andy McNab book for me in the basket.

Alex couldn't be persuaded to choose a book for himself, so off I went to see if there was anything else that caught my eye. After a bit of hunting around, I found the book *Catch 22*, which was included in the '3 for 2' offer. Being the classic it is I felt I had to read it at some point, so added that to our pile as a possible.

At the same time, mum spotted a book about France that she liked. Mum lived in Monaco for a few years in her twenties, speaks fluent French – when we go on holiday the locals thinks she's 'one of them' – and is passionate about everything and anything to do with France.

Unfortunately, I don't share her passion – don't get me started on France. The memories of those terrible evenings sitting at the kitchen table, desperately trying to fight the urge to tear up my French homework book and throw it across the room, hoping it would land in the kitchen sink.

Actually, I once gave in to the urge (but this time it was with my homework diary) and threw it across the room. It landed rather satisfyingly in a bucket full of water that mum was using to clean the floor. However, I remember making up some 'the dog ate it' excuse and my tutor just gave me a new diary. How boring, I could have at least received a detention.

So now we had four books and we only needed three. Ah it's OK, not a hard decision.

"Mum, put the Andy McNab book back and take your French book. I've read so many McNab books recently I can do without another." I offered.

"I'm not sure you'll read *Catch 22*, you didn't read that last classic you bought…" mum replied, picking her eyebrows – she always does this when she's nervous or can't make her mind up.

Using my body language book I deduct that by doing this mum is trying to 'see no evil' by covering her eye; she wants to close her eyes and for it to all go away.

What body language book? Why, it is the Bible of my book collection! Now please click this link to buy it from Amazon and earn me lots of money: **http://www.amazon.co.uk/referral=jellyellie**. Nah you don't have to do that, but I'll tell you what the book is. It's called The Definitive Book of Body Language by Barbara & Allan Pease. And I haven't been paid to mention it – I truly love it.

I've always been interested in trying to work out things from looking at people, and Derren Brown's acts employing mind reading are really impressive. I like psychology in general, but especially the focus on people, so this book on body language looked like a great place to start.

The book's not all great though: your family will hate you. They will *hate* you.

"Dad, uncross your arms! We can't have a sensible debate if you're biased like that."

"Mum, put your thumb and forefinger tips together rather than point."

"Come *on*! What have I told you about the effects of resting your head on your hand whilst having a conversation with somebody?"

And so on.

The amount of things you learn from reading a book like this is phenomenal. It opens up a whole new world; it makes you aware of actions that you've been using subconsciously all of your life, actions which you can now begin to control and use to your advantage in social, business and personal situations.

Funnily enough, however, one of my friends 'doesn't believe in it'. What is there to believe in? It's not like magic, and it's not like a religion. It's something one can educate oneself in, put into practice, and see the results in black and white. Yikes, did I actually just use the word 'one'? Awesome! I'm *truly* upper class now.

So, perhaps my friend was afraid of the new possibilities the book might open for him? Scared of realising that the negative body language he's been giving out all his life has had bad consequences? I wouldn't know… the only thing I'm thinking about is that cute guy I saw earlier… I'm sure he meant something when he was looking at me in that way…

 "…I think you should get the McNab one instead", came Mum's reply to my offer of swapping McNab for *Catch 22*.

"Uh, great, THANKS mum! Stop treating me like a child – I can choose which books I want to read! Oh no, not bright enough to read a classic…"

But mum was in no mood for arguments: she put down her French book and walked to the till to pay for the war book, Catch 22 *and* McNab's latest offering!

"No, mum! You have the book you want – I don't need two!"

But no, she insisted. Great. Two books; does that make me unwillingly spoilt? I don't want two! I wanted mum to have a book!

I still don't know why she bought me two books. It wasn't as if I deserved them. As Alex had complained, I had been annoying all morning, questioning everything mum said. It wasn't fair; I really didn't want that second book. Well, of course I *wanted* it, but I want lots of things and don't actually expect to get them.

Now, here's a great lead into the next chapter. I bet there's a phrase you can spot there that you often hear coming from the mouths of your teenagers: 'stop treating me like a child!'

2

Stop Treating Me Like a Child!

Introduction

Gain an insight into what we think about this controversial topic through an interview with a teenager. Learn how younger siblings can affect parents' judgments on the freedom they give their teenagers and how best to deal with this. Discussion on treating girls and boys differently with regard to going out by themselves, and the need to emphasize to your teens they need to earn the right to be treated like an adult.

I was surprised when I caught myself saying this earlier. It's not something I like to say; it's a bit of an immature protest, as it's usually just used as a single, unsupported phrase that does nothing but create arguments. I think the saying in itself, 'stop treating me like a child!' is a very uneducated thing to say (god I'm such a snob).

It's in this way that lots of teenagers say it without thinking – as I did earlier – and don't really mean it, and some say it to rebel against their parents and the way they treat them.

However, sometimes we really do mean it when we tell our parents to stop treating us like children. Even now, at 15, my mum is very protective over me; for example, she doesn't like me eating beef jerky when there's nobody in the house because I might choke on it and die. I understand that mum cares about me, but really that is a bit over the top.

Another situation where we may be forgiven for saying 'stop treating us like a child' is when our parents keep reminding us not to do daft things that we were told to avoid as eight, nine, 10 year-olds – don't jump into the road in front of incoming cars, don't talk to strangers, wear your helmet on your bike. I don't want to be hurt any more than mum wants me to, so it just gets annoying when our parents tell us not to do potentially harmful stuff that we wouldn't do anyway.

> When telling your teens not to do something potentially danger-
> ous, remember that your teens don't want bad things to happen
> to them any more than you do.

I know parents mean well when they say these things, but to teenagers it just comes across as if they have very little trust in our judgment – something that parents should avoid like the plague, as one of the most important things to teenagers is to feel that we are being treated like adults.

Now this is a very interesting point. We teens all want to be treated like adults, and indeed we all see ourselves as adults, but let's just think about it for a moment. Stop treating us like children? Of course our parents will treat us like children: we *are* children.

We might have boyfriends and girlfriends, drink, have our own bank accounts and travel abroad without our parents, but we're still only children. We teenagers are just a fifth of the way through our lives. We don't have the matureness, the experience, independence or the responsibilities that adults do.

So whilst one of the things that teenagers appreciate most is to be treated like adults, you still need to bear in mind that your teens are technically children.

> Despite whatever reasons your teenagers may give, remember that your teens are actually still children.

You can use this argument to show your teens that they need to *earn* the right to be treated like adults – they must realise that it's not something they are automatically granted the second they turn 13.

If my parents think that I don't deserve to be treated like an adult, they'll tell me straight out. This is just the way to do it, as I then have to think about what I could do to gain my parents' trust. I won't just be nice for a day and then stop because that's *such* an old trick and my parents know me too well to be fooled when I do that. It's worked quite a few times though [cough].

> Make it totally clear that your teenager needs to earn the right to be treated like an adult.

After speaking with friends, being treated like a child is one of the main things they say they dislike when discussing how they feel their parents treat them.

Here's an interview with a friend talking about the subject; you'll gather that it's pretty much unedited bar a few grammar imperfections, just as all interviews in this book are (I was going to star out the swearing to protect those younger readers, but I've always wanted to publish a book with a swear word in it).

jellyellie: Hi Kev! What have you done today?

Kev: Nothing.

jellyellie: Ah in the teenage spirit ☺ Now then, you have a younger brother don't you? How do your parents treat you in relation to him – do you get the same pocket money, chores etc.?

Kev: The same pocket money, not that it's enough for me to buy anything with. He does feck all, I'm made to do everything while he sits on his lazy arse whining!

jellyellie: Hmm, that sounds familiar. Now this might be pushing my luck a bit, but is there anything you appreciate about the way your parents treat you?

Kev: They couldn't care less about what I do.

jellyellie: In what sense – where you go and people you meet, or what you do with your free time at home e.g. computer/TV rather than something active (but of course there's nothing better than a good workout at our keyboards)?

Kev: Well, they wouldn't care if I started going out till god knows what time (they'd probably be glad to get rid of me!), and they aren't bothered that I sit here all day and night till whatever time I want (probably because I've left school).

jellyellie: A thorough answer!

Kev: Merci Boucoup. Beaucoup rather! Damn French spelling.

jellyellie: Indeed – well it's their turn to moan at us now: we won the Olympic bid! Now let it all out, what don't you like about the way your parents treat you as a teenager in comparison to when you were, say, 10?

Kev: It's not really much different. I still get treated like a child. My brother (who's 11 today) gets treated in the same way, if not better. He's not made to help people all the time; 'ooooh he's too little'. Well, how come those exact same words weren't said when I was his age?

jellyellie:...and when you were his age you had to help with stuff that he doesn't do now?

Kev: Yeap.

jellyellie: I think you'll find there's no 'a' in that word!

Kev: Yeap ;-)

jellyellie: Typical stubborn teen!

Kev: Yeap. Oooh that really pisses me off too! 'Oh you're just a typical teenager'.

jellyellie: Yeah me too!!! So, have we finished the interview then?

Kev: Now we have ☺

...so there we go. An interview with a REAL teenager! Yes – pure off the streets of England. Well, fresh off of my MSN list.

Forget those dreary interviews with middle-aged psychologists with sleeves full of qualifications and degrees; to get to the bottom of the whole teenage mindset all you need to do is talk to a few teens.

Isn't that amazing? You can *talk* to teenagers! But you didn't think they spoke...? Well there's proof they do and I didn't need a degree to come up with it. Try it yourself, folks. And put away those fags for god's sake, you don't need to bribe us, and definitely not with *those.*

> Talk to your teenagers, talk to friends' teenagers, talk to your nephews and nieces... we don't bite. Treat us like adults: we'll appreciate it and are more likely to act responsibly.

After talking to friends with younger and/or older siblings of varying ages, I've found out that it's normally the older child who complains about being treated like a child (i.e. me). After much thought and research, I've come up with a few reasons for this:

1 Their parents are so used to protecting their younger child that they forget the older one has grown up and doesn't need to be treated in the same way.

2 The older child is around their younger sibling a lot, but desperately wants not to be a child but to be a grown up teenager. The older child may complain of being treated like a child because they genuinely believe they are being treated like a child. Or the older child may just want to rebel and remind everyone how un-cool it is to be a child, and how everyone should treat them like a big cool teenager not a little kid like their sibling. Got that?

3 The elder child isn't 'overly' complaining of being treated like a child, it's just that the younger child doesn't complain at all because they've grown up with the whining of their older sibling and have seen how pathetic it is.

> Make sure you treat your teenagers according to their age and
> maturity, especially if they have younger siblings.

It's OK; I'm allowed to slate the older sibling like this – that was me
not so long ago, and the younger sibling in the third example,
that's now my brother, bless the little angel.

Indeed, it's interesting to see the difference between the way I'm
treated and how Alex is treated, regarding going out by ourselves
to meet friends, or just riding down to the shops on our bikes. Alex
is a boy, and he's quite a bit taller/bigger built than me. Whenever
he goes out, it's "Have you got your phone?"

"Yep"

"Where are you going?"

"To the park."

"OK. Be back before dark."

On the other hand, whenever I want to go out somewhere, it's
"Where are you going?"

"To James's house."

"Is his mum in?"

"No."

"Well, I'm not happy with that."

"That's stupid. We'll be going out anyway."

"Where?"

"To town."

"Be careful. Have you got your phone?"

"Yes."

"How are you getting there?"

"Riding."

"Oh no please don't… I'll give you a lift."

"No, I'm riding."

"No really, I'll give you a lift."

"No, I want to ride."

"Well make sure nobody stops beside you in a car and grabs you."

…all because I'm a girl. At first I thought it was sad that the world has turned this way, having to think about being abducted, raped and murdered when we go out, but actually, keen to do some research on the statistics, I found out that there are hardly any more abductions and murders today than there were when you – our parents – grew up.

The Home Office's British Crime Survey, based on incidents reported by surveyed members of the public, reports that in 1982 there were fewer than 2,250,000 violent incidents against adults – including teenagers aged 16–19 – in England and Wales. In contrast, this figure rocketed to 4,256,000 violent incidents in 1995. It has now fallen by 43% in a decade, as just 2,420,000 incidents of violent crime were reported to the 2005/06 BCS.

> The levels of murders and abductions are the same today as they were when you grew up – treat your sons and daughters accordingly.

I know you may have been a lot older than a teenager in 1981 (sorry) but unfortunately, as the BSC only started in 1982, the figures for previous years are unavailable. However, I think the figures available go to show that there is very little difference between the rates of violent crime today and when the majority of today's parents-of-teenagers grew up, and grew up with very different attitudes.

Back then, parents were keen to let their teens go out on their bikes for the day. No thought was given to the possibility of being abducted – and most teenagers didn't know what the word paedophile meant.

What has changed then? Have parents just become more cautious? No, the media has become more integrated in our every day lives. Whether it's listening to the radio whilst the kettle is boiling, updating our iPods with the latest podcasts, the plasma telly in the kitchen or the latest footie results texted to our phones, nobody can miss the latest news these days. And of course, everybody loves a gripping story to break the monotony of the rat race. The media are doubly sure to pick up on and exaggerate every possible murder, rape or abduction.

Homework:

○ Ask your teens if they think you're treating them fairly, and if there is anything they'd like you to do differently.

○ Treat your teenagers according to their age and maturity, especially if they have younger siblings. Give them tasks that require more maturity than jobs they used to do/jobs their younger siblings do (e.g. cutting the hedge with an electric cutter, doing the BBQ, cleaning windows up a ladder).

○ Tell your teens if they don't deserve to be treated like an adult. Make them work for your trust – they're still children so being treated like an adult is a privilege, not something to take for granted. Damn, mum and dad are really going to hold this one against me…

3

You're Spoilt

Introduction

I give you a real insight into what goes through our minds when you fling the 'you're spoilt' phrase at us, and some definitions of what I think a true spoilt teenager would equate to. How best to approach this subject with your teens. Illustrated by a real-life example of a conversation about being spoilt.

Another chapter, another real-life example. Isn't it exciting? I've just got home after walking back from a local music festival I went to with mum and dad. A music festival with my parents; am I mad? Probably. But I must admit, dad has a good taste in music most of the time. Except for Christina Aguilera, Britney Spears…hmm, I wonder why…

Of course, a heated conversation took place whilst walking home from the festival. What was the topic? Ah yes: I'm spoilt, apparently.

Now before I really get started on this, let me just clarify what I think it means to be spoilt:

The term 'spoilt' is normally used to describe a child who gets everything they want in a materialistic way. Think Veruca Salt from Charlie and the Chocolate Factory.

A spoilt child will sulk, scream and shout until it gets its own way. And yes, it's an 'it', not a he or a she; spoilt kids – *its* – are horrible things. They're doing nobody, especially themselves, any good. Rotten brats.

Now let me be blunt. These are examples of kids I'd describe as spoilt:

1 Child has TV, DVD player, stereo, Xbox and PS2 in its bedroom. Child asks mother for a Gamecube because he wants to play the new Zelda game when it comes out. Mother refuses. Child asks again. Mother refuses. Child has a tantrum. Mother refuses. Child sulks. Mother gives in and buys child Gamecube.

2 Teenage daughter wants a new bag in the sale. Parents say no, wait for your birthday. Daughter asks again. Parents refuse. Daughter screams at them. Parents refuse. Daughter threatens to drink all of parents' alcohol. Parents give in and buy daughter a bag.

As these examples show, being spoilt is not so much about class and wealth, but about parents giving in to their teenagers' demands and refusing to say no and really meaning it. Therefore, just because a teenager from a rich family has a car and flat paid for by their parents, they might have more than other teenagers, but it doesn't mean they're spoilt – their parents may regularly say no to requests for cash handouts, holidays with friends, and expensive parties in 5* hotels.

> Being spoilt is about how often you refuse to buy something your teenager requests, not about how many latest gadgets/clothes/shoes they have.

You may have begun to realise what this also means: the key to raising an unspoilt teenager lies entirely in your hands. It is up to you to say no.

> It's down to you to raise unspoilt teenagers by saying no and meaning it when your teenager repeatedly requests something.

If your teenager respects you, they won't ask again. If, however, they have no respect for your word and know they can keep pushing you until you break; well, that's where the problem lies – and the next chapter gives you tips for gaining respect so your teenager will respect your word, and hey presto, no more spoilt teenager.

So, I was walking home from the festival with mum and dad. We were talking about the music that was playing and dad commented that he wished he could play an instrument really well. He has a piano and has taught himself some blues but – in his words, honest guv – he's too old to begin learning an instrument. Mum agrees, and says I need to take full advantage of being able to learn an instrument whilst I'm still young.

At the moment I have an electric guitar and I'm teaching myself to play that. However, I would also like to play the bass guitar. I've wanted to play bass for quite a while now but have never really mentioned it seriously to mum and dad because I know what will come next…

"You're not having a bass guitar! You've already got a guitar. You're so spoilt; a bass!"

"Oh for god's sake! All I said was that I'd like to play bass."

"Bass! You've got a guitar; you can play that. Some kids have to save up for years and years to get a guitar, now you've got one and you want a bass too. You're just spoilt, Miss Ellie."

"Oh come on, I bought my guitar years ago! It's not like it's top-of-the-range, and it's not like I've constantly whinged for a new £400 guitar. No, I've –"

"Ellie, you do *not* need a bass too!"

"You're such hypocrites though! You say I should take advantage of being able to learn an instrument, and when I say I'd like to learn something new you launch into the whole 'you're spoilt' attitude. It's ridiculous!"

"It's not ridiculous. If you want to learn an instrument, you can play the piano."

"I don't want to play the piano! If you want to force me to play the stupid piano like every other parent does, then fine, but I'll just end up hating it and everything else to do with music."

"Fine, we'll force you to play the piano. 10 o'clock tomorrow morning, bright and early, you can start on that."

"Oh come on! That's not the point. I say there's something I'd like to learn and you just go into all of this! It's *stu*pid!"

…and so it continued, my parents going into detail about every little thing they've bought me – and me reminding them that I actually bought it myself, but that backfiring when they reminded me where I got the money from (them) – until we got home, and here I am now, writing. I love writing when it's dark and quiet. It's so… refreshing, and cosy. Definitely cosy.

Oops, back on topic.

> Don't say 'you're spoilt' without really meaning it: your teenager will take it to heart and a long argument will ensue.
>
> If you really do think your teen is spoilt, don't say 'you're spoilt', it's the most antagonising phrase ever.

So my parents think I'm spoilt because I have an electric guitar and I want a bass too. But, as I have described, I don't think this alone means I'm spoilt. I can see their point of view – I'm lucky to have an electric guitar and amplifier, and everything else I've got, and it just seems extravagant to have a bass guitar too – but actually, to really be spoilt, I would need to scream and kick and moan and whine until my parents give in and buy me a bass. And I'm not going to do that, because I know that's what spoilt kids do, and I don't want to be a spoilt kid.

But on the other hand… hah, you knew that was coming! On the other hand, if I don't learn the bass now, I'll get to dad's mighty old age and regret not learning it – especially as I've the motivation and inspiration to learn now.

So what shall I do? Well, the next thing I'll buy is a bass guitar so I'll just start saving [cough] and hope I can persuade mum and dad to put something towards it [cough]. Note: Persuade doesn't mean scream/sulk until demand is met. That's for spoilt kids, remember. No, persuade means… hmm… on second thoughts, let me edit that.

So what shall I do? Well, the next thing I'll buy is a bass guitar so I'll just start saving [cough] and hope I can ~~persuade~~ *encourage* mum and dad to put something towards it [cough].

There we go, that's better. 'Encourage' – much more of a not-spoilt word.

[Pause]

Wait, I just had a horrible thought. Maybe 'encourage' is just as 'spoilt' as 'persuade'; perhaps I am spoilt!

> We don't want to be spoilt… we know it's a horrible trait.

Well, whatever the answer, I feel I'm glad that I can at least see mum and dad's point of view. I can see why they think a bass would be extravagant and partly agree with them, but the majority of me disagrees. I'm not going to scream and shout and ask for a bass every day until I get one though, as that *would* make me spoilt.

I think deep down every teenager knows their parents have some truth to their words when they're called spoilt – perhaps not quite in the way of my two extreme 'spoilt kids' examples – but you must remember that being spoilt is a lot more than just having lots of nice things.

> If you think your teen is spoilt and discuss this with them, your teen may partly agree with you but won't admit this, so don't push your views too hard – chances are they do agree.

Because my generation has so many more personal possessions of real value than you did as teenagers – as my parents keep reminding me – this alone makes it easy to label us as spoilt, when actually we're quite average. As long as you remember to say no every now and again, you can allow your teenagers to keep their computers, TVs, Xboxes, wardrobes of clothes, stacks of shoes and racks of guitars, safe in the knowledge that, no, you're not raising spoilt teenagers.

Remember: Just Say No. God I hate that phrase...

Homework

○ Never say 'you're spoilt' to your teen. I don't know what it is, but the words 'you're spoilt' seem to be inbred in our 'words-to-start-an-argument-with-our-parents' list. We're just being defensive I guess.

○ Make a list of all the things your teenager asks you for over the next week, and make sure you say no – and mean it – to a good chunk of them. Tell your teenager why you're doing it; if they realise that pushing you into buying them something means they're spoilt, they might think again the next time you say no – we hate the thought of being spoilt.

Getting Our Own Way

Introduction

I discuss the relationship between having respect for a parent and getting your own way. I offer an example of this using my own parents – one of whom I have much respect for, the other I have less respect for – and discussing how this has affected myself and my brother. A selection of comments from friends on the subject of having respect for our parents. Example of a teen getting her own way and discussing why she succeeded.

The relation between this topic and the *You're Spoilt* topic, to use a phrase I don't like, is 'the same but different'.

'Spoiling' is most often associated with money and material objects, whereas getting your own way conjures up images of little kids lying on the floor screaming and kicking until they don't have to do the washing up, but really the two go hand in hand. Six of one, half a dozen of the other, that sort of thing.

Therefore, if a child/teenager is spoilt they're also very likely to get their own way, and vice versa.

> Being spoilt and getting your own way go hand in hand. If you conquer one issue, the other will follow naturally.

Before we go any further, here's a scenario I think you'll all be able to relate to. It's written by a friend of mine, **Zeth**, who went on holiday with his girlfriend Becky.

"We were on the beach, soaking up the sun and chatting. Well, all apart from Becky who was fixing her snorkel set. When she'd finished, she wanted her dad to come in the sea with her. Her dad didn't want to, he was eating some watermelon. But Becky wouldn't take no for an answer: for at least half an hour she sat on him, threw sand at him, pulled, pushed, and begged her dad to come in the sea with her.

I couldn't believe it. Her dad just didn't put his foot down – he was laughing at Becky, even though he was really quite angry with her. He was laughing because he couldn't think of any other way to deal with the situation. Becky saw him laughing and thought he was actually enjoying being pestered so she continued. I really could not believe it – her dad just laughed even more!

Eventually Becky and her dad went for a walk to the café, with Becky still trying to push her dad in the water all the way down the coast. How embarrassing. When they got back, Becky's dad gave in and went in the water with his daughter. 1–0 to Becky."

This whole situation came down to two key words: respect, and being consistent (OK that was four words). Becky had no respect for her dad because her dad wasn't consistent in his parenting methods; when he said no, Becky knew he didn't really mean it and she kept pushing him. It's incredibly simple: if the parent is consistent in his/her methods of parenting and punishment, the child will have respect for the parent.

> To make sure your teenagers don't get their own way, they need to have respect for you. Gain this by being consistent with boundaries.

I believe that whether a child gets their own way or not is mostly down to the parents. Their methods of parenting and type of discipline will determine how far the child thinks it can push its parents. For example dad is, and always has been, much more true to his word than mum. I suppose some people may think he's being strict, but really he's just sticking to his word. He lays down boundaries and my brother and I know that he'll be true to his word in punishments, so we have lots of respect for him because he never lies or exaggerates.

On the other hand, Alex and I rarely listen to mum's wishes because we know that any threat she makes if we don't do as she asks won't be carried out. However, we'll always do what mum asks if dad is within earshot. My poor mum, I must have knocked a good few years off her life.

Edit: Alex was very upset after he read this chapter, as he doesn't agree with the 'Alex' part in "Alex and I rarely listen to mum's wishes". I suppose I agree with him, so I must own up and tell you that Alex has always been a lot better behaved with mum – and dad – than I have been.

Therefore, the child's personality also plays a part – I used to be a right little so and so with my mum, but my brother was never as bad despite being brought up exactly the same as I was. So, it's not *all* down to the parents.

Now then, how does this all tie in to *Getting Our Own Way*? Well, this relationship I had with my parents meant that I would always ask mum for something, not dad. I knew dad would say no and that he'd really mean it. On the other hand, mum could always be persuaded to change her mind – yes, I could get my own way with her.

What the teenagers say

I spoke to some of my friends and asked them to comment in general on the subject of having respect for our parents. Here's what they had to say:

"I'd respect my parents if they stop thinking they know best, and perhaps treat me like I'm 17 not 12. And I'm sick to death of being told to cut my hair." – **Kev, 17**

"To get my respect, they could do something really stupid and funny, like walk down the street dressed as Ali G… or summin'…" – **Conor, 14**

"A teenager will NEVER respect their parents, it's a known fact. But if they were to gain respect, I guess it'd be by not embarrassing them whenever they go out." – **John, 16**

"Well I respect my dad more than my mum because my mum worries too much and is unfair about things whereas my dad is firm but fair." – **Caragh, 16**

"If they show me respect, I'll reciprocate the feeling." – **Ross, 17**

John's comment – "A teenager will NEVER respect their parents, it's a known fact." – was the one that stuck out the most for me. I guess if you were to ask every teenager in the country what their views were on this subject, John's answer would be the most common viewpoint, both the never-respecting-your-parents part, and the not-embarrassing-me-when-we-go-out part.

Wanting to see if that was really his opinion or whether he was just upholding the teenage views expected of him, I put it to him that it can't be true because I respect my parents. Now this made me laugh: he replied with "Same." So first we created a mutual teenage bond by saying how we could never respect our parents, but then I broke the convention and said I respect my parents. John then realised that he does too actually, so he had to reveal that he wasn't being entirely truthful in his original comment.

So of course, it's convention amongst teenagers to say how they could never respect their parents because they just totally don't have a clue, maaan. But actually, if one teenager says they *do* respect their parents, then everybody else hops over the fence and comes clean too.

> Don't be offended if your teenagers say they have no respect for you. They're just trying to fit in and uphold the teenage viewpoint expected of them. No matter how anti-mainstream or individual your teenagers are, they will always be affected by peer pressure.

The second part of John's comment, "But if they were to gain respect, I guess it'd be by not embarrassing them whenever they go out.", is another thing commonly stated by teenagers. But it's funny, because it could be seen as totally contradicting Conor's statement: "To get my respect, they could do something really stupid and funny, like walk down the street dressed as Ali G". So is it acceptable for our parents to publicly embarrass themselves, and us, or not?

What John was talking about was situations when our parents insist on coming somewhere with us where we're likely to be seen by people we know. When this situation occurs, parents don't seem to get the hint to go and hide until the friends have gone, but tend to do things that teenagers find embarrassing. It's hard for parents to know when to walk away in these situations because they may not realise that just saying hello to our friends constitutes felony number one. We're very emotional creatures and tend to overreact in situations like this.

> If you're out with your teenager and their friends approach, hide. Hide in a very dark corner.

On the other hand, Conor was talking about situations where our parents are so embarrassing they're cool; but so embarrassing to *themselves,* not to their teenagers. Take, for example, my dad. He loves to put on this funny waddling duck walk when out with us in public. It's absolutely hilarious – he's being cool and acting like a teenager, not the 21-year-old he is (he bribed me to say that, he's really forty-.....oops no. I'm being bribed again).

> Act cool once in a while – do silly things that only teenagers would normally do… but use your judgment to make sure they're cool, not embarrassing.

Caragh's comment, "Well I respect my dad more than I respect my mum because my mum worries too much and is unfair about things whereas my dad is firm but fair," backs up exactly the point I'm making throughout this chapter.

As you may have noticed, I've not really spoken about 'getting our own way' much in this chapter dedicated to the subject. Instead, I've gone on (and on, and on, and on) about gaining respect. This is because I believe this is the only way to make sure they don't turn out as spoilt brats who get their own way all the time. So concentrate on this, and bringing up teenagers who don't get their own way will come hand in hand.

Homework

○ Gain respect from your teenagers by being consistent with any punishments. This week, if you threaten something, make sure you carry it out. It will be hard, but your teen will start to see you mean what you say, and you will be able to continue doing it for years to come.

○ If you're out with your teenager and their friends approach, don't say anything to your teen or his friends whilst they're talking.

○ Go and put some dog poo in a paper bag, set it on fire, leave it on your neighbour's doorstep, ring the doorbell and run away. Just make sure your teens are watching – they'll be damn proud to have you as a parent.

Money and Jobs

Introduction

A general chapter on money including discussions on allowances, my thoughts on giving teens allowances, how to get your teens to find a job, and an interview with a friend covering drugs, arms dealing and prostitution. Mmm can't you just taste the juiciness? Another subject that closely ties in with being spoilt, money is something that comes into nearly every argument in our household.

As a child I was given £2.50 pocket money a week – when my parents remembered to give it to me, that is. My brother is 16 months younger than me and we always got the same amount, and started receiving pocket money at the same time. Of course, I always complained that I should have an extra 16 months' worth of pocket money to catch up with the extra that Alex received because of this, but my luck never caught on.

Now, at 15 years old, I haven't received any pocket money for years – neither has Alex. This wasn't due to a conscious decision by our parents to stop it, or to give us an allowance instead, but it just gradually wore off. Instead, mum and dad buy bits for Alex's remote control cars, and dad pays for my website hosting/domain names, so that makes up for our missed pocket money more than enough times.

> If you don't give your teens pocket money, support their hobbies instead.

I mentioned allowances: some kids, when they reach their teenage years, are given allowances. I'm sure you're familiar with allowances: when parents give their teens a lump sum every month (around £50) and they have to buy everything they want. I say want, not need – parents will buy them a new pair of trainers when *needed*, but if the teen *wants* a designer brand they'll have to pay the extra out of their allowance. The same goes for clothes. Everything else – leisure activities, cinema, CDs, computer games, magazines – also has to be paid for by the teen out of their allowance.

> If you give your teen an allowance, set out strict rules for what they have to buy themselves.

When I first pondered on the subject of allowances a few months ago, I thought that an allowance was good in the way it prepares teens for when they have to budget for themselves, but I thought it created a very false sense of security and is expensive for parents.

Also, as a teen, I understand that even if I wash the cars, clean the house etc. and my parents give me money, I become 'richer' but my parents become 'poorer'. Therefore, no money has been added to the overall household income, it's just changed hands. Instead, I want to actually bring money into the house by earning it myself from the outside world. This will benefit us all at home: I'll have extra money, and my parents won't lose any by giving it to me so they can spend it on nice things – like TVs and holidays – that will again benefit us all (hah-hah I wish).

> Try and get your kids to realise that the whole household will benefit if they earn money from the outside world rather than live off pocket money from you.

It's on this basis that, a few months ago, I thought I would never give my kids an allowance; instead I would encourage them to work outside the household to earn their money. However, as I have travelled a little further into my journey of teenager-hood, I realise that this is not the only thing to think about when it comes to allowances.

Recently, dad and I have been having lots of 'discussions' (read, arguments) about money. Because there are some things my parents are happy to pay for when I go out – lunch, a £10 phone top up once a month, train tickets, books – I am forever asking them for money, giving change back, asking for money, giving change back… and sometimes I will use my own money for things like lunch and ask my parents to pay me back later.

As you can well imagine, this gets rather higgledy-piggledy:

"Where's that tenner I gave you last week?"

"What about lunch – you never paid me back!"

"Did I ever get the change from that £10 I gave you for town?"

"I paid for my top up last month as well!"

So, how does having an allowance come in to this? Well, I think that if my parents gave me, say, £20 a month for things like lunch, train tickets, top ups etc. and said 'that's all you're getting', we wouldn't get into any of the mess we're in at present. In this sense, I would be receiving a sort of 'leisure allowance' – my parents would still buy my clothes, shoes, etc. when I need them, but the allowance would be a good idea to stop us getting confused with money constantly changing hands. Better still, if they did it as a direct debit into my account, they would never forget, and there would be no cash changing hands whatsoever. Perfect.

> If you find yourself constantly owing each other money try giving your teens a tailored allowance.

Now then, what sort of things do my parents buy me? What am I made to pay for myself? Well, here's a good example: my guitar. I bought my electric guitar and amplifier out of my own money. When the strings break, dad will buy me new ones (£5.99 for a set).

When we were in the guitar shop the other day, buying yet *more* new strings, I mentioned that I could do with an electronic tuner. The cheapest one was about £15. Dad pondered for a bit, obviously trying to think of a reason why I didn't deserve it – it was futile, I knew he'd say yes. But on what conditions?

We struck a deal: I'd pay half. After speaking to the assistant about my constantly breaking guitar strings, we chose a thicker gauge but were advised to bring my guitar in and get it set up properly for a princely sum of £35. Dad immediately made it clear that I'd be paying for that.

That little example sums up the sorts of things my parents will buy my brother and I:

○ We pay for big things ourselves (e.g. guitar and amplifier, £100).

○ Mum and dad will buy smaller items of maintenance (e.g. guitar strings, £6).

○ We'll go halves on more expensive but beneficial things (e.g. tuner, £17).

I think that's pretty fair overall, but I do believe that parents should contribute to their means towards big items of an educational benefit, such as a guitar. As I go on to mention in the "Hobbies and Interests" chapter, if parents are worried about their children starting lots of expensive instruments, they could strike a deal along the lines of: child pays for instrument at the outset to show commitment, then if child sticks with it for set amount of months, parents will pay for half.

Here's an interview with my friend Carl, who also plays the guitar. I've interviewed him about money, the sort of things he has to buy, if he gets any pocket money, and – mum and dad this is for you – if he had to buy his own guitar. We also touched on jobs towards the end.

> **jellyellie:** Hi Carl!
>
> **Carl:** Good day kind woman! OK, OK, hi Ellie!
>
> **jellyellie:** Don't you think we tend to overuse exclamation marks a bit these days?
>
> **Carl:** No! They are awesome!
>
> **jellyellie:** :-D

Carl: But not used in their original context anymore; just thrown in randomly at the end.

jellyellie: I've been using them very sparingly in my book.

Carl: Yeah I don't like them in books. Makes the book seem wannabe cool.

jellyellie:...and if you read a 'classic' where they don't use many, the effect is amazing when they do put one in.

Carl: Uhuh. Because I read all too frequently...

jellyellie: Hehehe. Well, we were supposed to be talking about money, so let's cut to that.

Carl: Yes. Money. OK.

jellyellie: You're an avid guitar player. Who bought your first electric guitar for you?

Carl: My parents, as a birthday gift.

jellyellie: You did better than me then. I paid for it all myself! Did you have to pay a contribution?

Carl: None.

jellyellie: You just end up hating some people... Err yes. So, what about strings, picks, other consumables/loseables etc.? Who pays for those?

Carl: Most of them are paid for by me, but some exceptions occur.

jellyellie: OK. And do you have to pay for that out of pocket money, money you earn from a part-time job, or what? ...drug dealing, prostitution...?

Carl: Uhmmm, miscellaneous funds and rarely drug dealing. And selling myself. And arms dealing. Err, forget the latter two...

jellyellie: Damn, I was after a nice Glock 17. So you don't get any pocket money on a regular basis, or an allowance?

Carl: Nah, random cash injections.

jellyellie: Now that is an idea I could introduce my parents to. So are you going to be looking for a job soon?

Carl: Not that I know of, summer job maybe. Still only 14 though Ellie...

jellyellie: So definitely not a paperboy?

Carl: Hell no! Unless it was like the late route... and people enjoy waiting for their papers...

jellyellie: :Haha! Yeah, I tend to agree. OK. I think that's probably all for now, unless you have anything to add relevant to the subject of money?

Carl: Hmmm... nope.

jellyellie: OK. You know, you should savour this moment... not long you'll be looking back on a printed version of this in my best-seller book... ah those will be the days...

Carl: Hahaha :-D

jellyellie: I'm not lying! It will happen. I think, however, if we go on for much longer I'll have to increase my word estimates for each chapter. Hokay. Interview terminated at 22:58.

So as you can see, Carl doesn't receive any set pocket money or an allowance, just like me. However, he doesn't have a job either, which isn't like me.

At the moment I'm working for BT, as a columnist for a new website that should be launched shortly. It's damn cool – whilst everyone at school is off doing work experience, I'm sitting in a meeting on the top floor in BT Centre in London!

I'm definitely not doing it just for the money though; apart from the fact that I love writing, it's an invaluable experience to have and the contacts I'm making are worth more than their weight in gold.

As well as writing for BT when their new site is launched, I've just imported a load of laser pointers from a manufacturer in China to sell on eBay. Now that was an experience.

> Encourage your teens to earn money for themselves. It doesn't have to be a conventional job – eBay is a great place to learn basic business skills.

My ultimate goal in life is to own and run a successful multi-million pound business. Every day I make sure I do something productive that will take me one step closer to that goal, and every day I envisage myself as that bigwig exec with a penthouse in London, a big house right on the sea, a pad in Monaco, and a 100ft yacht sailing around the Med. That *will* be me.

I'd also like to be successful with my writing; if you are reading this, I've obviously made it somewhere in the world of publishing. Has it been a big success yet? I'm sure it will be. I'd like to write further books after this one, and continue writing freelance like I am with BT.

When my dad was a teenager, he lived on a boat with his family for three years and they went sailing around the Mediterranean. Unfortunately, it's an expensive way to live, and mum and dad haven't been in the position to do the same with Alex and me. I would love to be able to live with my kids on a boat for a few years, as the experiences it opens you up to are amazing. It makes you stronger as a person and as a family, you make so many good friends, and it gives you a level of independence you'd never get from living on land all of your life.

> Errr… live on a boat if you can afford it!

Writing would be a perfect way to sustain a suitable income for me to be able to live on a boat – you can write from wherever you are in the world. Hopefully, if I make enough money soon enough, I will be able to take my mum, dad and brother on a boat for a few years, as it's dad's dream to live on a boat again.

So enough with the motivational and dream stuff: what you want to know is how to get your damn lazy teenager off his butt, out of the house, and working.

Well… I'll tell you how not to do it.

> "I had an absolutely blazing argument with my dad the other day. My parents have gone and filled in a load of job application forms for me for shitty places like Sainsbury's, Tesco and crappy Woolworths. What the hell do I want to work there for? Maybe if they actually speak to me about getting a job, and help me apply for one at a place where I'd actually like to work, I might be

> a little more motivated about getting off my arse and earning myself a living. As it is, they've totally blown it, and there's no way I'm going for any job interviews now." – **Calen, 16**

Cal hit the nail on the head there. If you want us to get a job, it's no good nagging and moaning at us to go for an interview at the local newsagent or supermarket. Instead, the motivation for working must come directly from ourselves – and I hear you cry "What! My teen will never take the initiative to get a job himself. If all my nagging hasn't made him get one, I don't know what will", but that is where you are wrong.

If you want your teenager to get a job, and he's shown no signs of going about this himself, what you should do – and what Cal's parents failed to do – is have a discussion with your teen and try and come up with a few places they might like to work. If they're obsessed with computers, they'll be far more excited and motivated about working in PC World than Morrisons. And if they're always bashing away on their drum kit, help your teen apply for a job at a local music store.

> If you're desperate for your teen to get a job, the motivation needs to come from them – help by discussing where they would enjoy working. Whatever you do, don't force your teen into getting a job.

It seems like really simple stuff, but as Cal's situation demonstrates, it can be so easily overlooked when parents are just desperate to get their teens out working.

So you've well and truly conquered the money subject now. You know whether to give your teens an allowance, you know what sort of things you should expect them to pay for themselves, and you know how you're going to get them to earn that money from someone other than you.

Homework

○ Make sure you're giving your teens monthly pocket money rather than weekly as it encourages them to plan their finances and not waste it on rubbishy things each week.

○ If you're not giving your teens any pocket money, let them know you'll support their hobbies instead.

○ If you give your teens an allowance, set out strict rules for what they have to buy themselves. If you don't do this, the whole 'responsibility' side of having an allowance goes down the drain.

○ Contribute towards things of educational value as much as possible. Instruments, ice hockey gear, and web design software – it all counts.

○ Encourage your teens to earn money for themselves. It doesn't have to be through a conventional job – help them start an eBay business, for example.

○ If you want your teens to get a job, the motivation needs to come from them – help by discussing where they would enjoy working.

Fashion

Introduction

I discuss what it is about the average teenage mindset that makes us want to spend money on a little logo. I give you a top-secret guide to what different brands mean to teens, and how you can recognise what image group your teen belongs to.

I'm sitting here in my £45 Fat Face hoodie and £8 pair of cotton trousers from the hippy market in Camden, London. The two couldn't be further apart in terms of price and brand: Fat Face is an expensive, upmarket brand aimed at middle class men and women with an adventurous outlook on life. Their clothes are hardwearing and capture the whole outdoors image, and Fat Face sponsors surfers, wakeboarders, windsurfers, rock climbers, mountain-boarders etc. all round the world. The hippy trousers… well, to be honest, they look like a pair of pyjama trousers. Thin, baggy, and very stripy. You know the sort.

Apart from being worn by surfers and the like, Fat Face clothes are now commonly worn by Innocent-smoothie-drinking, vegetable-growing, organic-food-eating women who live in suburban towns and cities. So why do people in cities need hard-wearing, out-doorsy type clothes? Well, they don't – just as your teenager doesn't need those £80 specialised Nike running shoes for school

PE, or those £75 skateboard shoes for hanging around in.

Everybody buys clothes for the image and style they represent, and nobody does this more than teenagers. It's terribly important for us throughout these years to try out different identities, feel like we 'belong', and find our own self-image. The easiest way of doing this is by carefully selecting the brands and styles of clothes we wear.

Here are the main 'groups' your teenagers might fall into, identified by nothing other than the style and brand of clothes they wear:

Group	Common Brands	Clothes styles	Shoe styles
Emo	Converse, Vans, Von Dutch, Heartcore, Atticus, Dickies	Very tight jeans, stripy long sleeve tops/jumpers, zip-up hoodies, 'trucker' (mesh) baseball caps. Lots of black, red, and stripes. Guys (and girls) wear bright pink	Converse All Star baseball boots, old-school Vans slip-ons
Goth/metaller	New Rock, Criminal Damage, Underground, Dr Martens	Long black trench coats, baggy black trousers with straps. Metallers wear heavy metal band t-shirts	Big chunky high-leg leather boots with metal buckles. Mega-high platform shoes
Chav	Nike, Adidas, Reebok, Puma, Umbro, Ecko, lecoqsportif, Patrick, fake Burberry	Sports clothes – tracksuit trousers, zip up tracksuit tops, hoodies, fake Burberry items, baseball caps, thick fake gold chains	Expensive sports trainers

Grunger	Hoodies with band logos, Criminal Damage, Vans. Not much branded stuff	Ripped jeans, band t-shirts and hoodies, dad's old shirts over t-shirts, bandanas	Skate shoes, Dr Martens boots
Skater	Vans, DC, Globe, DVS, Element, Emerica, Adio, Etnies, Osiris, Dickies	Baggy jeans and combat trousers, t-shirts, hoodies, polo shirts, Beanie hats and trucker baseball caps	Big fat chunky padded skateboard shoes (yummy)
Surfer	Vans, Animal, Billabong, Reef, Mambo, Weird Fish, Oakley, Fat Face	Baggy combat trousers and shorts, baggy hoodies and t'-shirts, sunglasses, 'boardshorts' in the summer	Skateboard shoes or sandals
Hippy	None – at a push, fair-trade brands such as Namaste	Baggy, cotton, hemp, very casual, earthy colours, 'flowy' materials. Fair-trade stuff from Nepal, woolly jumpers	Simple canvas/ cotton shoes, sandals or skate shoes
Fashionistas	Top Shop, New Look, FCUK, Ted Baker etc	Whatever's fashionable – jeans, skirts, tops, cardigans, handbags etc. all in the latest fashion	Shoes in the latest fashion, whether it be ballet pumps, wedges, or chunky lace-ups
Normal	Top Shop, New Look, Next, Adidas	Jeans, zip-up tops, t-shirts	Normal shoes and trainers, skate shoes

Chavs have suddenly become proud of being called chavs. This isn't good if your teenager is like this: chav is a word with very bad connotations.

Only the hardcore emos don't mind actually being called emos. Emo stands for emotional punk (a genre of music), and you should keep an eye on your teen if they fall into this group, as they often talk a lot about suicide and being depressed and cutting themselves.

There are so many different groups I could go on and on for hours, but that's not necessary; the groups listed above are the main ones that teenagers go for these days. You'll probably be able to identify which style your teenager subscribes to.

As I was doing some research online to find out what sort of brands some types wear, I came across a few posts on some music forums. Inevitably a member had posted a question like "Do your clothes reflect your choice of music?" and (s)he had been flooded with replies such as "I don't care what clothes mean, I just wear what I like.". This is what all teenagers like to think – me included – and some genuinely do try and be like that. Others just say it because nobody wants to admit they belong to a group and follow like sheep: we all want to be individual.

Even the anti-mainstream groups these days (emo, goth, grunger, skater, surfer, hippy) all have a dress code you abide by, so really there is no getting away from conforming to a certain dress.

Even the most anti-mainstream groups have dress codes.

Here is an interview with Josh, who is a proud member of one of the most anti-mainstream groups – he is a goth/metaller.

jellyellie: Hey I'm writing a chapter on clothes and stuff, can I interview you as a goth/metal type?

Josh: Hmmm…. You've asked that before…Yeah sure!

jellyellie: Coolio! OK, well it's not a formal interview. Just us chatting here on MSN.

Josh: Dammit no Ellie in a suit then.

jellyellie: Hah! You'll never see me in a suit.

Josh: Why not?

jellyellie: Because I'm never going to have a job where I need one, and I'm not going to wear one when I run my own company. Quite simply.

Josh: What about a wedding? Or will it be a nice dress for Ellie then?

jellyellie: Yeah! A dress.

Josh: I wonder what you'd look like in a wedding dress.

jellyellie: Very white I'd imagine. I bet you'll wear your trench coat when you get married – and I bet it will be longer than your bride's dress!

Josh: Yeah, probably. And it'll have a red velvet lining.

jellyellie: Coolio… so why do you like wearing the clothes you wear – trench coat, black jeans, big New Rock boots?

Josh: Black.

jellyellie: But... in that case, you could wear a black Nike track-suit.

Josh: A black leather tracksuit???? I like black, leather, and studs.

Josh: And boots.

jellyellie: OK cool – but why? Because it's associated with the type of music you like, because it's what your heroes wear, because it makes you fit in with your friends? Why?

Josh: Because it's related with the music I like and because it makes me stand out.

jellyellie: Cool. And nice name! [Josh had changed his online tag to "Let's kidnap Ellie and dress her up in a wedding dress!"]

Josh: Lol, thanks.

jellyellie: Here look, my name! [I'd changed my name to "...and let's put Josh in a red velvet-lined wedding trenchcoat – but not to get married to me!"]

Josh: Lolol! Remove the last bit, and see which of our friends notices first.

Josh wants to see me in a wedding dress. Should I worry? Oh, wait, that's not very relevant.

So Josh likes wearing what he does because it's part of the whole scene he's into. He also likes it because it makes him stand out, and it certainly achieves that. I guess it's important to stand out these days because so many teenagers look the same, subscribed to one of a few main groups. If you're in a less popular group (goths, grungers, hippies), you're bound to stand out.

And now, (after your homework – which I hope you're still doing), onto that very subject: standing out from our peers.

Homework

○ Go to your local town for a spot of sightseeing and see if you can identify a few of the abovementioned style groups.

○ Try and guess what sort of group your teenager fits into by using the above chart. Don't tell them you know what group they belong to, however – they'll be offended and complain that they 'don't belong to a group'.

P.S. Josh's girlfriend was the first to notice our MSN names, she told Josh off twice.

Crazy Shoes

Introduction

In this chapter I use my crazy shoes as an example of how I'm different to everyone else and love being this way. I talk about the lack of individuality amongst teenagers and how it's not cool to be different. However, sometimes things can be so different they're cool – just like my crazy shoes.

In the true spirit of creative writing, I'm going to imagine a random possession of mine and describe it in the most detail possible.

Now, what could I describe... hmmm... my favourite top? My phone? Nah... I know! My CRAZY SHOES!

Despite their simple canvas construction, I paid (well, mum paid) £45 for my crazy shoes. This must mean only one thing: yup, they're branded. They're easily identified as Vans by the big white leather 'V' sewn into the side of them. This white 'V' is as synonymous with skaters as the Nike 'tick' is with chavs. The V is easily seen against a background of the brightest, most striking pink canvas you could ever imagine. There are black suede sections on the back of the shoe and around the lace holes to protect the canvas in vulnerable areas.

The shoes are 'old school hi-tops' so they have no padding and just a simple rubber ridge around the bottom of the shoe. As I turn the shoe over, I see a traditional waffle sole commonly found on classic Vans skateboard shoes.

I suppose I should be referring to them as boots not shoes; the canvas extends up the wearer's leg about 8", but the top can be rolled over a few inches. When it is rolled over like this, a black and white chequered pattern on the inside of the shoe is revealed, heavily contrasting and complementing the bright pink canvas. To top it all off, I have exchanged the normal white laces for a pair of one-inch-thick fluorescent pink laces. They're so bright that even against bright pink canvas, they made the shoes look pretty dull for a while until they got a bit grubby too.

And finally, imagine a bucket of mud thrown over the shoes, the soles heavily filed down by sandpaper, and the rubber ridge around the shoe peeling away from the canvas. Ah yes, they've been well used – from May 2005 to February 2006 these were the only shoes I would wear. They've been to London numerous times, to Portsmouth, they've been to Turkey, Belgium and Menorca. They've been on trains, on tubes, on aeroplanes, in cars, on bikes, on skateboards, on mountainboards. They've been to the beach, to parties, to music festivals, to exams, to posh lunches, to the London Book Fair. They've been in the sea, they've flown my kite… they've been everywhere; it didn't matter if they didn't go with the clothes I was wearing, I *had* to wear my crazy shoes.

Why? *"I thought girls were supposed to have lots of shoes and be totally indecisive about which ones they wear"*, I hear you say. Well, indeed you are right. I have about 20 pairs of shoes (see I'm a normal teen really), but for eight months I wouldn't wear anything other than these shoes. Sure, a few times I stepped out of the door with a different pair on because they looked better with my outfit, but I quickly ran back inside and put my crazy shoes on.

I love them because they're crazy, totally unique; I think I only ever saw one other person wearing them. When I wore them out and about, people always came up to me and asked where I got them from – middle aged ladies loved them the most. So yes, I loved the attention. They always, *always* drew looks. It was a way for me to show people I'm different, a way for me to stand out from the crowd.

I would never go anywhere without my crazy shoes as they were an easy way for me to say "Hey, look at me! I'm an individual, not a run-of-the-mill teenager!" and I love being different. So it allowed me to fit in and wear normal clothes – clothes categorising me in groups – but at the same time show people how I'm not the same as everyone else.

> Your teen might wear outrageous clothes to show people they're individuals, not normal trouble-making mainstream teenagers, as we're generally perceived to be by society.

Different groups have different attitudes towards individuality. Some actively promote it and the whole anti-mainstream thing (e.g. goths, hippies), but for groups like Chavs, if you're not wearing the latest pair of Nike trainers then apparently you're a total loser.

But these days, even the most anti-mainstream groups have pressures within their groups to wear certain clothes and listen to certain music.

> Your teen will have different attitudes towards individuality depending on the "group" they identify with.

In schools anti-individualism is rife amongst students and teachers. The whole education system does nothing to discourage this, as teachers can't cope with individuals – you must all be the same for the system to work. If you don't fit in with the rest of the kids in your class, you're automatically labelled as a troublemaker or a geek depending on which end of the scale you fall off. Anyway, more on the crappy education system and how you can encourage your teens to do well in the School chapter.

> Anti-individualism is rife in big schools so keep an eye on your teen if they're in this environment.

Now, sometimes things can be so different and terribly uncool they are actually cool. Don't ask me how this works... if I told you, I'd have to shoot you, as I'm sure it could be a very lucrative secret: imagine selling your grandma's old, uncool clothes in London boutiques for hundreds of pounds an item! OK, so it's not really like that, but just as my friend John illustrated that "respecting your parents is so uncool that it's cool", lots of things have come back into fashion now after being seen as the most ludicrous, uncool things ever. For example, a few years ago it was all the rage for 'grungers' to wear big baggy jeans and hoodies. All of a sudden, those same people – now turned 'emo' – are wearing the tightest jeans you could imagine. Perhaps one day somebody's mum shrunk their jeans into drainpipes and they had nothing else to wear when going out with their friends. Perhaps the teen felt like a right twit going out wearing them, but because they were *so* different to baggy jeans, they were a hit with their friends.

> Trends often switch to radically opposite fashions, as these are the most outrageous compared to existing ones.

It's the same with my shoes. Because they're not just a little bit different, because they're so outrageous, my peers take it as an opportunity to say 'hey, that's cool!' If they were just a little bit different (like a pair of old-school-style Nike trainers with a pink tick) then people would just think I'm sad and I didn't fit in. However, because my crazy shoes are so totally unique, my peers took it as an opportunity to embrace something radical, therefore proving they weren't just sheep who only like normal things. Of course, an ironic effect ensues: everyone starts to like the new trend because it's anti-mainstream, so everybody buys into it, copying each other. The original reason for the trend becoming popular because it was something unique is totally out of the window by then.

> Things must be totally different to be perceived as "so uncool they're cool".

Wait a minute, have I just worked out how trends start? Wooooooh I'm a geeeenius.......... (not).

Homework

○ Google for a picture of a pair of shoes matching the description I give (they don't have to be the same colour). Email it to **crazyshoes@ellie-g.co.uk** and I will let you know how you got on. Being able to identify popular shoes will gain you respect from your teenagers!

P.S. I no longer wear my crazy shoes as 'emos' have started wearing the same style of canvas Vans old-school trainers. Although they don't wear the same colour as mine, I no longer like to be seen in my crazy shoes because they're not different enough to the ones the 'emos' now wear. Hopefully the emos will switch to something different soon and I can get my crazy shoes back out.

Names/Nicknames

Introduction

Most teenagers will go through a period of hating his or her given name and wishing to be called something else, myself included. I discuss why I went through this, and how I'm just beginning to like my 'old' name again. Interview with a friend who uses a totally random nickname.

I was outside on my skateboard the other day when two boys who live down the road came out with their football. Alex and I used to play with them quite a lot, but we haven't seen them for a year or two now. We kicked the ball around for a bit, then someone booted it up the road and I went to get it. Jack, one of the boys, shouted something like "Eleanor, haha, Eleanor!" because the last time I spoke to him – well over a year ago – I would have gone mad if anyone called me by that name.

So there you go, the truth is out. I know you all think my real name is 'jellyellie', but unfortunately my parents aren't *that* cool, and my name is actually Eleanor.

Indeed, from the age of 0–11, everybody knew me as Eleanor. However, in those last couple of years at primary school (age 9 –

11), I played football with all the boys at breaktime. Soon, 'Eleanor, pass the ball!' became 'Ellie, pass the ball!' – much easier to say.

When I started secondary school I fancied a change, and introduced myself to everyone as Ellie, and that has stuck ever since. It took a while for my parents to get used to calling me Ellie, but I forced them to comply and went absolutely mad whenever someone called me Eleanor – I absolutely *hated* it.

Below, I explain to my grandad, Pappy, why I decided to make this change.

> **Pappy:** Why is your name Ellie? When I went to the doctor's I told him to look at your website, and I said to refer to you as Ellie not Eleanor; parent-given names aren't allowed!
>
> **jellyellie:** Quite right too. I didn't like being called Eleanor because people couldn't pronounce it –
>
> **Pappy:** Oh! That's interesting, I hadn't thought of that.
>
> **jellyellie:** – yeah, some people said 'En-ner'!
>
> **Pappy:** Oh!
>
> **jellyellie:** And I suppose I didn't allow people to call me Eleanor because I wanted to be different and break free from my parents.
>
> **Pappy:** Makes sense.
>
> **jellyellie:** Well, actually… I was thinking about going back to Eleanor because Ellie's too common now.
>
> **Pappy:** Well, there you go. But at one stage you couldn't stand being called Eleanor! Was that because it was too common?

So I originally went from Eleanor to Ellie because:

○ I wanted a change – I love change.

○ Ellie is shorter than Eleanor, so easier for my friends to say in hurried situations – football, running from the police, etc. (joking on that last one).

○ It made me pull my hair out when I was "En-ner".

○ Finally, Ellie was a nickname. Everybody wants a nickname! Oh god… that reminds me. At one point I chose the hideous nickname 'Spike' for myself, purely because I wanted a "nickname". I'll get my coat now…

> There are legitimate reasons for teens wanting nicknames – their given name may be too long or too hard to pronounce, or too embarrassing.

But – yes, you read correctly – a few months ago, much to the bemusement of my parents, I decided I liked Eleanor again. Ellie *is* becoming too common, and Eleanor sounds/looks much better with my surname than Ellie does. So when I sent out the proposals for this book, I decided to become Eleanor. It was extremely weird receiving emails and letters addressed to "Eleanor", and I started to wish I had just stayed with Ellie, but I have come to like my old name again.

> Like many teenagers, I used to hate my real name and chose a nickname. However, I'm now starting to go back to my real name.

Even though I prefer Eleanor over Ellie, all of my current friends know me as Ellie and I can't see that ever changing. I also can't imagine ever introducing myself as Eleanor to new teenagers I meet, and it's dead weird when my parents call me Eleanor – dad only does it very rarely when I've done something wrong and he shouts without thinking.

I deliberated long and hard over what name to put on the front cover of this book. If I was going to put my proper name, I would definitely put Eleanor not Ellie. But no, it had to be jellyellie – forget Ellie and Eleanor, jellyellie is a far cooler name and *everybody* knows me as that; I'm not Ellie or Eleanor, I'm jellyellie.

jellyellie really is my ickle trademark. It's not a new creation, though – I thought of it with my friends from primary school when I was 9 or 10, and created my first email address **jelly_ellie@hotmail.com**.

So, I wonder how my friend 'Chip' got her nickname, and indeed, why she prefers it to her parent-given name of Sophie…

jellyellie: Hi Chip!

Chip: Hello!

jellyellie: So, can I call you Sophie – or will you go mad and insist on being called Chip?

Chip: Either's fine.

jellyellie: Do your friends call you Chip and your parents/relatives call you Sophie? Or do you have one group of friends who call you Chip, and another who call you Sophie?

Chip: My family call me Sophie, and some friends call me Chip; it depends how I met them I suppose.

jellyellie: Yeah. So, why "Chip"? Do you like chips??

Chip: Well a friend of mine made it up one day, it was kind of random. There's not really a story behind it – sorry to disappoint you!

jellyellie: Hehehe, OK. Did you just want a nickname then?

Chip: Yeah, I hated my name since I was young. At primary school I had another nickname but once I got to secondary school it sort of died out, so I got another one.

jellyellie: Ah right! And do you still hate your name?

Chip: Nah it's alright now, if I meet new people now I'll introduce myself as Sophie.

jellyellie: Yeah, why do you think that is? Not rebelling against your parents so much by using the name they gave you?

Chip: It wasn't about rebelling; I just didn't like my name. Now I've just got used to it; it's only taken 15 years! I guess I realised I've got to like it 'cos I've got it for life.

jellyellie: Uhuh, cool. I like Sophie BTW.

Chip: Thank you

jellyellie: S'ok! So I think that about concludes our little interview, unless you have anything else to add on the subject?

Chip: Nope that's all I think.

jellyellie: Coolio! Thanks Chip.

And to round up this chapter, here's what another friend had to say on the subject of nicknames, which was rather more concise:

> "I used to be called 'Ferdie' sometimes, but personally I prefer 'Lord of F'ing Darkness!!!!!!!!!!!' – Freddie, 12

Homework

○ Ask your teen if they would like you to call them by a shorter form of their name, or a nickname, etc.

○ Tell your teen the nicknames you used to have – go on!

School (Sucks)

Introduction

What you should know about school.

I talk about why school doesn't suit a lot of teenagers, how this is overlooked and turned into 'Damon's so naughty and disruptive', and how you can help your child if this is the case. Why it's important to find your child's learning style, how to get your teens to go to school, get good GCSEs, and do their homework.

For those parents who have tried absolutely everything and are at the end of their tether, I offer another option you might not be aware of.

School, eh. Now this is something I have quite a few strong opinions about. Firstly, I'll explain what situation I'm in when it comes to school.

I went to primary school for the full seven years and, despite refusing to leave mum and dad in the mornings for the first few years, I really enjoyed it. The teachers were fantastic, I had loads of friends, I was academically pushed in class, loved the family atmosphere and generally had a great time.

Then I went to secondary school, supposedly the best comprehensive in the county – so say the results tables, anyway. And yes, we were one of those middle class families who moved house to get in. It's OK though, we got our 'served you right'…

After the first year or so the novelty of a big school wore off, and I began to hate my time at secondary school. Very few of the teachers knew my name, we weren't allowed to mix with kids outside of our year group, there were constant disruptions in lessons, and the system didn't allow us to be pushed to our limit.

As you can already guess from the fact I'm talking about it in the past tense, I don't go to that school any more. I left at the beginning of Year 10 to be home educated, and that's what I'm doing now. It's fantastic; the freedom is amazing. You don't have to stick to timetables or the national curriculum or take any exams, and it's definitely not just for freaks and geeks – I have joined local home ed' groups and there are real, normal, home educated teenagers. I could go on for pages after pages about why it's so good and how I'd recommend it, but I'm sure that wouldn't help you get your teens to pass their GCSEs and do their homework, so that's enough for now.

> Check out home education if you're looking for an alternative option to the school system.

◎

I was walking up to the shops the other day during school time and saw an old friend from primary school, Tom, bunking off with his mates. Just before they rode off on their scooters around the neighbourhood, I had a quick chat with Tom, asked him how he was doing and what he was up to. He was OK, totally fed up with school, the 'normal' sort of thing.

It made me really upset to think that lots of my old friends were like this now, bunking off school, hanging around totally bored with crap GCSE predictions.

The sad thing is all those friends did so well at primary school; they were liked by everyone and had good relationships with the teachers. Now, school is their worst enemy; the teachers unforgiving; lessons dull; and coursework piling up. They don't know where they're going in life and will probably be incredibly lucky to leave with 5 A–C GCSEs (not that you need qualifications to succeed in life, but more on that later).

I don't want to sound like I'm putting myself above these teenagers, because I'm sure I would be exactly like them if I hadn't have left school when I did. I'm extremely grateful for the opportunity I've had, and wish other teens could have similar opportunities – I'm not saying all teenagers should be home educated, because that wouldn't suit everyone, but we should all be allowed to learn in a way that suits us best.

My point is, these once-happy kids have been transformed into naughty, bored teenagers. Sure, some people will just blame it on our parents or adolescence, but I don't believe that. I think that the failure of the education system to cater for students as individuals has contributed to these teenagers' attitudes.

If your teenager is failing at school, ask yourself – even better, ask them – what the reason might be. The problem may be with the school, not with their 'teenage attitude'.

Now you may take that as a cue to accuse me of being one of those people who encourages parents to go against the school system and have a go at the headteacher every time their little Shayne or Aisleyne gets a detention for swearing at the teachers, but that's not my point.

What I'm saying is that school doesn't suit a lot of people, but especially the most academically challenged and the most academically apt. These kids are at the extreme ends of the scale, the ones who would benefit most from an individual education; something nobody will truly get in the school system.

> Fact: school doesn't suit everybody.

I have a theory that these kids at the extreme ends of the scale generally tend to be OK at primary school because there are fewer pupils, so teachers can cater to their needs more individually. However, when they enter secondary school, they get lost in the system and are expected to conform. Inevitably they will get frustrated that they're either too far behind or not being pushed enough, and they'll vent their anger through means such as disrupting classes, bunking off school or bullying. Then they're labelled troubled kids, and expected to fail from then on in life.

> If you feel your teen is especially bright or finds academic work difficult, make sure that appropriate provision is being made for their needs at school.

My theory is all very well, except for one slight flaw… the opposite can also happen: bright/challenged kids sometimes prefer secondary school over primary school because the bigger school has the resources to help them, as my friend **Rich (now 20)** found:

> "I really disliked primary school because the school itself was awful. The headteacher refused to admit any problems with the school, even denying there was bullying when my mum showed him my school shirt with other kids' footprints on it. The head then referred me to a child psychologist because I was disruptive in lessons. The psychologist concluded that I was a fine, bright young child, and I was so disruptive in school because I was bored with the unchallenging work. Again, the school refused to accept the problems lay in its hands, and did nothing to stretch me academically. I enjoyed secondary school a lot more, despite it being a large school with over 1,600 students. Even though we were working towards SATs and GCSEs I didn't feel that I was being spoon-fed things to learn like I was at primary school. We had access to textbooks and libraries, and the teachers were more than willing to help us with any extra-curricular queries."

Therefore, it goes without saying – the school you choose to send your child to has a massive influence on how they enjoy their time there. If you're currently in the process of choosing a school for your child, don't go on results tables alone.

Whatever you do, it's extremely important that your teenagers feel you are on their side. Don't contribute to school brainwashing by calling them lazy, rude, or failures. People are only lazy when they are unmotivated, and a bad school or failure to encourage your teen is exactly what will cause a lack of motivation.

Instead, understand what it is that's making your teen act the way they do, and see if there is anything you can do to solve it. If they feel they're struggling, the best thing to do is talk to them and really listen, understand how they feel. Don't just say 'OK well I'll get you a private maths, English, science and French tutor' because that's not going to help. Your teen might be behind because they don't learn effectively by reading textbooks and answering questions. They might prefer to get their hands dirty doing things and experimenting practically – this is called a kinaesthetic learning style, which isn't an approach used in normal maths, English, history, French etc. lessons at school.

Therefore, your teen may hate school just as much as the aforementioned bright/challenged kids do because their preferred learning style isn't an approach used in schools. The school system is based upon the visual and auditory learning style, which is no good if your child learns best with a hands-on approach.

> Your teen may be unhappy at school because their learning style isn't an approach used in schools.

This brings me to another important point: find out, at the earliest possible stage, how your child prefers to learn. There are lots of different tests available; there's loads of information online, and your child's school might even be able to help. This is probably the most important thing you could do to help your child's education.

It's extremely useful to know how your kids prefer to learn. One benefit is direct: when your child brings home homework or projects, you can sit down and help them choose a way of getting to the end product by using a method they favour. Once you know how your child learns best, inform their school so they can tailor their education as much as possible (hah yeah right). The more parents who are aware of different learning styles, the less it can be ignored by the government, and the more they will have to do to change their inflexible education system to make provision for these different styles.

> Get your child to take a short test to find out how they like to learn best and explain to them how this can help them learn more effectively.

Now, let's come to the subject you've all been waiting for: how to get your teens to go to school, get good GCSE/A-Level grades and do their homework (and absolutely anything else you want them to do – get them to clean your car, tidy their room, mow the lawn etc. Yes, this is a whole book in one chapter). Not that I believe in getting 10 GCSEs... but I'm sure you've already heard enough of my liberal views on schools, so I'll make my argument short.

It consists of two points: the first is that GCSEs and A-Levels are a farcical excuse for 'education'. Indeed, Dictionary.com defines the word education as *"the act or process of imparting or acquiring general knowledge, developing the powers of reasoning and judgment, and generally of preparing oneself or others intellectually for mature life."* How anybody can truly believe that four years of learning facts to pass exams is a suitable education to prepare for life beyond school is much beyond me.

Now you may be thinking, what a snob – everyone needs to take exams if they want to get anywhere; if my teens want to get into college, to University, and into the jobs they want, they need to take these 'farcical' exams.

Well, actually, here's my second point: GCSEs are completely unnecessary for getting into college – I have just received an offer to study A-Levels and I only have one B-grade GCSE – and likewise, a study has shown that many Universities will accept home educated students without A-Levels as they recognise qualities other than exam results. Of course, if you don't have GCSEs and A-Levels, you do need something else of equivalent stance to show colleges and university, so this isn't an easy get out for any teens reading who can't be bothered to sit their GCSEs.

But, I know, as much as you'd like to believe all that, GCSEs and A-Levels are the most practical way for your teenagers to come away from their education with some good results and get the job they want. So let's get started – how to make them study to pass those exams.

Now, unlike all the other parenting books, I'm not going to give you a list of things like 'ground your teen until they've done all their homework' and 'drag your child out of bed in the morning' because, quite frankly, that's wrong.

It's wrong because it won't make your teenager respect you, and as I have said time and time again, respect is the ultimate thing that will help you to be a good parent. Instead, when you walk out of the room after criticising your teen about their detention for no homework, they'll swear at you under their breath and just do the minimum required on their work so they can get it done. Your teen will have no pride in their work, as they won't have any respect for anybody's opinion on it – especially yours.

If you criticise your teenager without clearly demonstrating how your criticisms are very fair comments, they will have no respect for you or your opinion on them and their work.

Instead, you should show your teen sincere appreciation about the good things they have done; maybe they got a better mark than usual on a piece of classwork, or filled in their homework diary correctly. Even if their lack of homework, multiple Cs and Ds and poor school attendance heavily outweigh the few good things they have done, it's important to show appreciation rather than criticise. Then if your teens know you are going to show them some appreciation, they will want to do things – like doing their homework and getting good grades – to gain your appreciation again.

> Show your teen sincere appreciation about the good things they have done, however small. They will begin to respect you for not criticising them, and crave your appreciation even more.

I know it sounds rather basic and trivial and like it would never work, but actually the feeling of importance and appreciation is widely regarded, but most often overlooked, as one of the most basic human cravings; equal to the need for food, health, sleep and money.

Psychologist Sigmund Freud said that everything we do can be attributed to two motives: the desire for sex (parents stop giggling at the back) and the desire to be great – synonymous with feeling important. John Dewey, a highly regarded American philosopher, also believed that the "desire to be important" is the most important feeling humans crave.

> Banish those 'oh my teen will never respond to appreciation' thoughts. The feeling of importance and appreciation is widely regarded by well-known psychologists as one of the most basic things humans (yup, including your teenagers) crave.

Concentrating on your teen's good behaviour rather than their bad behaviour is a bit like what I do when I'm writing this book. I have moments when I get stuck and think what I've written is rubbish; oh yes, I have lots of those moments. But as I've gone on, I've learnt that instead of concentrating on the bits I hate and thinking how crap they are, I read back over the bits I've written that I really like. It puts me in a happier mood and reminds me of that great feeling I'll get when I rewrite the bit I'm stuck on and it turns out well.

So, yes, your teens will have lots of moments when they're falling behind with their grades and homework, and maybe skipping school. But if you recognise when those moments are, instead of criticising them, go and show them some appreciation about something else they've done well, no matter how small. They will like that feeling, and desire to do something else good so they receive even more appreciation from you. Easy, really.

> Concentrate on the good rather than the bad, and the bad will soon disappear. Well, to a certain extent – if you concentrate on having well-behaved teenagers a stork won't fly down and exchange your unruly ones for angels…

Homework

○ Ask your teen if (s)he is happy at school. If the answer is no, ask your teen what (s)he doesn't like about school. It may be that these problems have been overlooked as a problem with a teenager, rather than something the school could help with/improve.

○ Ask your teen's school if they could provide a test on learning styles for your teen to do. Inform the school of the results and make sure that as much as possible is done to cater for your teen's learning style. If nothing can be done at school, at least ensure you do your best at home to make sure your teen learns through the approach best suited for them.

○ Think of one thing you like about your teenager, and go and tell him how much you appreciate this right now. You might get an odd look, but if you keep this up – rather than concentrating on bad things your teen does – your teen will begin to respect you for not criticising them, and crave your appreciation even more.

○ If your teen isn't an academic whiz-kid, find out about work experience or apprenticeships they could take part in rather than encouraging them to go back and retake poor GCSE results. Your teen might be much more intelligent than 'academics' in ways not measured by normal qualifications.

○ If you are at the end of your tether and your teen is desperately unhappy, consider the home education option. As a parent you don't need to be a teacher or to have any formal teaching skills, and it's totally legal – the law only states that children of compulsory school age must receive a full-time education appropriate to their age, ability and aptitude. That's all; there are no curricula you must follow, exams your teens must take, or regulations to follow.

A good place to start is **www.education-otherwise.org**.

I'm Bored – Hobbies and Interests

Introduction

...the phrase every parent dreads, whether it's in the second week of the summer holidays or in the car to Auntie Doreen's. What you can do to encourage your teens to be proactive in doing things that are useful and interest them, rather than wasting time watching TV or trying to finish that excruciating level on Half-Life 2.

It's coming to the end of the first week of the Easter holidays. Right now, this very second, Alex is sitting in front of the TV watching... one second, let me go and see what he's watching... he's watching The Simpsons. He has already done the 'morning rounds' of his favourite car websites, and spent an hour or so playing driving games on the computer.

> It's OK to spend time on the computer to further an interest, but it's so easy to waste hours online.

Alex could quite happily spend the whole two weeks watching TV and going on the computer; in this sense, he is a typical teenager.

But on the other hand, and to give him credit, he has a hobby that he's really focused on: his radio controlled (RC) cars.

This gives him something constructive to do which builds his skills, concentration and self-discipline, and gets him meeting other enthusiasts on online forums, and in real life when they meet up locally. Dad supports Alex with his R/C cars – he helps him when he needs help, and will drive him to 'meets' when the forum members meet up in real life. Dad also buys little bits for Allie's cars sometimes.

> Support your teen's interests and help them with their hobbies. Even if you don't know anything about their hobby, two heads are better than one.

I think it's vital for teenagers to have a hobby they really love and are encouraged to follow by their parents. It gives us something useful to do with our time, and develops many other skills that will be useful in life.

> Encourage your teen to have a particular hobby that gets them focused and doing something productive with their time.

Saying that, I don't have a hobby I'm mad about – instead, I have a broad interest in lots of things. I love trying new things, and my parents encourage this. Although it's generally a good thing to try lots of new things, it can be very annoying and expensive for your parents. One week I'm mad about something and I've made my parents buy all the gear, and the next week I don't want to have anything to do with my new hobby.

If your teen has a bit of a track history like this, tell them it's good to try new things, and in general you're happy to support their hobbies. However, because their mind changing can be expensive, they will have to buy the initial equipment themselves – maybe you can pay 25% towards it. Then it's down to your teen to stick with it if they don't want to waste their money.

Yes, it will probably take them quite a while to save up for their new hobby, but this is the whole point. It will show you if it really was just a passing fad and your teen can't be bothered to save after a few weeks, or if they're totally focused and want to save as much as they can no matter how long it takes. If they then stick with the hobby, tell them that you will be happy to support them financially (pay for a guitar lesson, football team membership, memory cards for their camera etc.).

> If your teen tends to try everything and move on to something new every week, explain that this is a good outlook to have, but it can be expensive so they will need to save up to buy the initial equipment themselves.

If money is a particularly tight spot for you anyway, you may find it hard to support your teens with all of these weird and wacky hobbies. It's important to note that there are lots of hobbies out there that require minimal or no regular cash injections, for example:

○ Cycling – decent bikes can be had new for under £99, or second hand for a lot less.

○ Skateboarding – a complete board can be had for around £40 and requires no upkeep except for new wheels or bearings every six or 12 months – these cost around £20 to replace. There are no fees to use them – streets are free – and it's often fashionable to have a well-worn skateboard deck.

○ Guitar – new electric guitar packages including amps can be found on the internet for under £70.

○ Crafts – it may be a little different to skateboarding and electric guitar, but it costs nothing to collect scrap from around the house and garden and make artistic things. Your teen may even be able to sell their creations for a small amount – recycled things are very fashionable at the moment.

Indeed, as well as fun hobbies like football, guitar or whatever else, you should encourage your teens to do things to help their futures. If they want to run their own business, help them set up an eBay shop. If they want to be a fashion designer, buy them some material to make clothes with. If they want to be a professional musician, let their band practice in your house.

> Encourage hobbies that will give your teens a head start for their future.

However, if your teen wants to be a psychologist or something, you're unlikely to get them to study after school for a psychology GCSE not offered at school – the last thing teens want to do after they come home from school is do more work.

It's in this same sense that after-school clubs aren't always productive places. I've been going to a music club that starts at 4pm at a local school, and the kids who go to the music club who also go to that school muck around a hell of a lot. The professional musicians who run the club reckon it's because they're still in their school uniform; they've spent a day at school already, and they just want to go home and watch TV. However, when the same musicians run the club at venues like Youth Centres and Village Halls, they say the kids are a lot more productive. Because they've had to go home after school, get changed and think, "Right, I'm now going to a music club. It's not school, it's something I've chosen to do and will enjoy", they're much more productive in the sessions.

> After school clubs aren't always very productive as your teens are still in the school mentality and just want to get home. Instead, get your teen interested in clubs run later in the evening or at locations other than their school.

Getting back to the Easter holiday, boredom in school holidays is often a sour sore point between parents and teenagers. So far, neither Alex nor I have said 'I'm Bored', because dad has taken us to a few places and we have generally been keeping busy. However, it's only by luck that dad is around and able to take us to places – he's just finished his contract so he doesn't have a job. If dad had a job, we wouldn't have gone out for the past few days, and I'm sure Alex would be bored by now.

> If you're not able to be at home in the holidays with your teens to take them to their friends houses and such, at least give them some extra freedom (and money?) so they're able to use public transport, be independent and travel to see friends by themselves.

Homework

○ The second you finish reading this, go and ask your teen if there are any hobbies they would like to take up – mention old ideas which you previously turned down: ice hockey, in fear of broken bones, or paintball, disapproving of guns.

○ Tell your teen you will financially support their chosen hobby as much as possible, but if they tend to start lots of new hobbies then give them up, let them know that they will need to show the dedication first by buying any equipment needed and sticking with it for a while.

○ Let your teen know that you're happy for them to spend time on the internet (websites and speaking to 'strangers' on forums and MSN) furthering their interests. See the Internet chapter (next) for more info on how to manage this.

○ Find out if there's an alternative to the drama/football/music/swimming club at school, as after school clubs aren't always very productive because kids are still in the school mentality and just want to get home.

○ Are you reading this in a school holiday? Make sure you've given your teens a little extra pocket money for bus/train trips so you don't have to be a taxi for the week.

The Internet

Introduction

Using real life examples of experiences I've had with the internet I advise parents what to do when it comes to the internet and teenagers.

Parent: "Who are you talking to?"
Teenager: "Oh, nobody."
Parent: "Come on, who is it?"
Teenager: "Just someone from the internet."

I think those must be the most common four lines of conversation found in the average household with teenagers today. The most worrying thing is, it almost always stops at that forth line.

It stops here for a few reasons. You may:

1 Not be bothered about knowing whom your teens are talking to ('It's just the internet, nothing genuinely good or bad will come of it').

2 Want to know more but are unsure of how to approach the subject.

3 Know you are unlikely to get a straight answer, either because your teenager feels you will be judgmental about the answer, or else (s)he just wants to wind you up because (s)he knows how much you worry.

Whichever reason applies, none is good enough for an excuse. You need to talk to your teens about what they do online – not only to make sure they're safe, but to show them you take an interest in their lives and friends.

◎

The other day, whilst I was cooking some pasta for lunch, I thought that for this chapter it would be good to interview a parent about their concerns over their teens using the internet. I was thinking it would be interesting to find a 'typical' parent to interview – somebody with conservative views about computers, and who doesn't really know what their teens get up to online. I thought of one of my friends, Kev, who I actually met online and has since become a good real-life friend.

Whilst my pasta was cooking, I asked Kev if I could interview his parents. What was his answer? *"No, because then I'd have to tell them who you are, and they don't know you exist!"* In fact, not only do his parents not know I exist, they don't know that he has travelled for two hours to meet me six times, came to my 16th birthday party, and has stayed the night at my house. So even though Kev's response was bad because I won't be able to interview his parents, it also illustrates the precise point I'd like to get across:

...lots of parents don't know what their teens get up to online.

(Also, if you have a 17-year-old son called Kevin and you live in the south of England, maybe you should have a word with him.)

As parents you must take a genuinely interested role in your teenager's online friends. Talk to them about the websites they visit, the forums they belong to, and the friends they've made. I talk about my online friends with my parents, just as my brother tells dad about the latest news on the car forums he visits.

> Take an active interest in your teenager's online activities.

Not only is this good practice to ensure your teen's safety online, but you may find you quite enjoy hearing about the new friend your son has made in France; how they talk to each other in French, great practice for your son's up and coming GCSE. Perhaps that 30-year-old fashion designer your daughter has been talking to on the London Fashion Forums has been of great help to her, giving her tips on the latest fashion and recommending ways to get into the industry.

> The internet has a lot of benefits. Try not to be too judgmental of the people your teens talk to – "He's HOW OLD?! 30? He might be a PAEDOPHILE!!!"…much more likely he's not.

The best thing you can do is throw yourself in and really get involved. If you're not sure of how to best approach the subject, say to your teen something like "Oh, Mary at work was telling me how her son speaks to people online all round the world. It sounds really interesting – you must know people worldwide?"

There's an incentive there for your teenager to answer: (s)he's got to answer and boast about how many people (s)he knows from around the world as (s)he doesn't want to be put down against Mary's daughter who *obviously* knows *loads* of people.

> Give your teen an incentive to answer your questions – they've got their ego to think of and they'll never want to be put down against other teenagers.

Carry on the conversation; say how much you would have liked it if you could have had that opportunity when you were a teenager. Even if something strikes you as a bit dodgy – they mention the word 'hack' or '46 years old' – whatever you do, don't start going on about how they must make sure they're safe online and blah blah blah… zzzZZzZZZzZzzZZz… until you've read the section later about that stuff.

Most of all, you need to trust your teenagers. If you're all sneaky and install lots of monitoring software and parental controls, your teens will try their hardest to flout your restrictions, and be very likely to meet up with online friends behind your back, and that's not what you want – you want them to tell you about their online friends, and ask you if they want to meet somebody.

> Don't install lots of monitoring software and parental controls. This will just encourage your teens to be sneaky.

Because dad trusts me when I'm online by letting me have unrestricted use of MSN, forums, chatrooms etc. and have my own website, I know that I can go to him and tell him if something is worrying me on the internet. If dad had, for example, banned me from MSN, I would never talk to him if I felt uncomfortable about something someone had said to me on MSN because I know he would be cross with me for going on it in the first place. Instead dad trusts me to be sensible online, and in return I tell him if some weirdo starts talking to me or somebody threatens to hack my websites.

> Trust your teenagers when they are online and they will talk to you if something worries them.

As I mentioned in the previous chapter, the internet can be a fantastic way of furthering a hobby. Let's take Alex again, for example. He loves his remote control (RC) cars – especially Tamiya models. One of his favourite online haunts is the RC Car Club website, where he discusses anything and everything to do with Tamiya RC cars. Some of his online friends from RC Car Club have sent him free parts for his cars, given him bargain prices for upgrades, and given him help and advice.

He has now become an 'old hand', and in turn is proud to help the new members ('newbies') with his newly found knowledge. Whenever Allie gets a new RC car or does a new paint job, he sets the car up on some rocks in a flowerbed in the garden, takes a few photos and uploads them to his gallery on RC Car Club. He has even graduated to strapping Dad's video camera to his RC cars and filming action from the driver's seat – much to my Dad's alarm. The galleries are the most 'happening' places on RC Car Club, with members continuously commenting on others' photos and videos.

To make the transition from online to real life friends, Dad has been taking Allie to regional meets where RC Car Club members run their Tamiya cars together. He has met 20, 30, 40, 50 year olds. He has met bankers, IT professionals, freelancers, mechanics, and teachers. These are people that Alex, 13, would never in a million years go up to on the streets and start a conversation with, yet they have become his friends. They swap news on their RC cars, tell each other stories about paint-jobs going wrong, and talk about their lives in general. Alex has learnt so much from these people, and is a well-rounded person because of it – not many 13 year olds get the opportunity to have friendships and engage in mature adult conversations like this.

It has also given Alex the chance to learn so much more about Tamiya cars, as being such a niche hobby without the internet he would never find similar enthusiasts living locally that he could talk to.

As you can see, the internet can open up worlds never previously accessible. Teenagers with niche hobbies can get in contact with other enthusiasts from all over the world, sharing information and gaining knowledge they'd otherwise not have access to in their local areas.

> The internet is a fantastic way of taking part in niche communities, researching a hobby, and meeting new people.

So then, what if your teens want you to take them to meet people they've met online? I expect if they asked you this yesterday, you would have gone mad and said absolutely not – that's if you were lucky enough for them to ask you in the first place.

I have already outlined the benefits of allowing your teenagers to talk to 'strangers' online – making new contacts that might help their future careers, and furthering hobbies – but what are the benefits of meeting these people in real life? Why shouldn't they just take the low-risk option and carry on conversing online?

Well, I can go one better than just answer those questions: I'll tell you about the experiences I've had when I've met people online. *Note: It would be valuable if you can get your teenagers to read this next section, as a personal story from another teen might strike a chord with them.*

I was 13 when I first met somebody from the internet. At the time I was running a successful website dedicated to bluejacking (read more about it in the Preface at the beginning of this book) and had been asked to present about the subject at a conference in London. Two people from the forum on my website decided to come down to the conference and meet me. This was an ideal situation to meet people in: I was in a public place, my dad was with me and knew I was meeting these people, and I had known the two friends for a couple of months. Throughout those two months we had chatted publicly on my forums and spoken privately over MSN.

As always, I hadn't told my friends where I live, the school I went to, or my surname. These are just a few of the rules I always stick to when I talk to people online, no matter how long I've known them for. In fact, my friend Kev who I mentioned earlier, has only just learnt what my surname is; that's after two and a half years of knowing me.

Never reveal simple details such as your surname or town; this is common sense that everyone knows, but it's easy to slip up when you have known someone for a while and feel proficient with the internet.

I realise how important it is to keep these sorts of details out of the public eye after an encounter with somebody who managed to get their hands on them. Unfortunately, when I first launched my website, you were able to see my address under the registration details for the site. These have since been removed, and we've been careful not to allow this to happen with other websites we have registered, but at the time a not-so-nice-person copied down my surname and address. He has since taken a picture of my road name and local school on the internet and circulated these photos to other members of my forums. He'll probably read this, so I won't slag him off because I know he'll just email me saying he's getting his lawyers on me. What a twit. Oops did I just...? Oopsie!

> Search on Google for your full name, phone number, address and any other personal details – even partial digits of your credit card number – and see what is available about you online.

Drifting off topic slightly, as you can see I've had my fair share of weirdos. However, I haven't let it ruin my enjoyment of the internet; in fact it has been extremely valuable and educational.

I now know that anybody can start out normal then turn all weird, hence why I remain extremely vigilant about revealing my personal details. I've learnt that I need to be more careful than I ever thought I needed to be when it comes to hiding my personal details online.

More than anything, I've realised what horrible people there are out there in the real world. That's an important lesson to learn: it might scare you when you first encounter someone weird, but the earlier you learn about it, the wiser you'll be. It's not good to think,

"Nobody will ever stalk me… that stuff doesn't really happen," because you'll be all stuck-up and won't take proper care with being safe online. On the other hand, it's not good to be so petrified of being stalked that you never go online. Instead, strike a balance between the two: realise that there *are* weirdos out there, just like there are strange people who walk past you in the street. Be aware of the details you put in the public domain, and don't ever drop your guard when speaking to 'friendly' people online. If something bad does happen, it will scare you at first, but talk to somebody about it and learn from it. That's important: don't regret it and blame yourself for dropping your guard, but learn from it.

> There are weirdos out there, as there are out on the streets. It's important to strike a balance between becoming complacent and being too scared about weirdos.

What have I gone and done now? Just as I was persuading you to take your teens to meet their online friends, I've gone and put you off the internet completely! Well, let me try and change your mind again… let's go back to that story of meeting my online friends for the first time ever.

As I said, I was in the most-commonly recommended environment for meeting people you met online… public place, with an adult, etc. Dad was with me when I met my friends, and he enjoyed their company too. After the conference, we spent the rest of the evening together, heading to Leicester Square for a meal (and, for a laugh, walking round with napkins stuck to our shoes; great idea dad) and then making our way to the train station together.

Because I felt comfortable as dad was around, and because we met in a safe environment, we all had a thoroughly enjoyable evening and we met again a while later.

> Remember: make sure your teens meet people in a public place with an adult.

That was just the first experience of many, I have since met a plethora of online friends in real life. One friend flew over from Ireland, another came from halfway up the country. Some have stayed the night, and I have travelled far and wide to meet people too.

Meeting people in real life only strengthens the relationships you have built up online; I have made lifelong friends, invaluable contacts, and tonnes of fantastic relationships.

> Meeting online friends in real life is a great way of making an online friendship seem a lot more real.

All of these meetings have turned out brilliantly, and you can make sure your teens have the same great experiences by following these simple steps:

1 Make sure you go with them when they meet people.

2 Check how long they have known the person; the shortest time length I've met someone in has been a couple of months, and this worked fine. A few weeks is probably a bit early, but don't insist your teen has to know the person for *years* before they're allowed to meet up.

3 Don't impose limits like 'You must be 18 before you can meet someone' as, apart from being pointless, this encourages your teen to be sneaky and go off behind your back.

4 Become genuinely interested in how your teen and their friend met, so you can join in conversation too.

One final tip I have is to be proactive and ask your teen if there's anybody they would like to meet up with from the internet. This discourages your teen from being sneaky – if they think there's no way you'd let them meet people from the internet, they might just go off in secret and meet people without even asking you first.

> Be proactive – ask your teen if they want to meet someone from the internet.

Homework

○ Ask your teens about their online friends. Use the "Mary's Daughter" scenario to persuade your teenagers to give you a reply.

○ Remove any monitoring software and parental controls from your computer and let your teen know you have done this.

○ Ask your teens if there is a website or forum they would like to subscribe to that would help them with their hobbies. If you can afford it, subscribe for them now – otherwise these make excellent birthday/Christmas presents. This shows you understand the benefits of the internet and are willing to support your teen's hobbies.

○ Ask your teenagers if there is anybody they have met online that they would like to meet up with in 'real life'.

○ Google your full name, phone number, address and any other personal details – even digits in your credit card number – and see what is available about you online. If there is anything you think needs to be removed to protect your teen's safety online, contact the website owner (normally **webmaster@websitead-dress.com**). If it could be a serious threat to your teen's immediate safety, or you have found your credit card number on a dodgy list, contact the police immediately. They are very good with issues concerning the internet.

Computers and Technology Speak in General

Introduction

Know the difference between Apple and Microsoft? Between a chatroom and a forum? Do you know what your teen means when they say "BRB" or "WTF"? And, what on earth is a VoIP program? A short, sweet and simple guide to basic technology, internet speak, and other stuff that will help you communicate with your tech-savvy teens.

So, you have a computer.

As far as you're concerned it's just a box of wires and electronic bits that sits under your desk. It has a big blue button that you press to turn it on, and then pictures start appearing on the screen in front of you. Microsoft Word is great for writing letters to long-lost relatives; you check your email occasionally; you might browse eBay for a bargain or two; maybe you even download the pictures off your new digital camera.

Ask your teenagers what they use the computer for, and they'll start spewing out words which you've never even heard of, let alone know what they mean. Let's see…

What do I use the computer for? Well…I talk to my friends on MSN, I update my website with DreamWeaver and an FTP program, I belong to some forums, buy and sell on eBay, and do my work on Word. Sometimes I use PhotoshopCS2 to edit photos, I use VoIP software occasionally, and I update the mp3 collection on my iPod using iTunes. I built my own computer, and it runs a dual-boot of Windows and Linux. I recently got a TFT and we've always had cable broadband – it's just been upgraded to 3mb. Of course, I also love to bluejack people.

You're probably thinking: "WHAT? Could you please repeat that in English?"

So, here you go… a guide to common phrases and what they mean. Now, go and impress your teenager looking *smug*.

General Technology Terminology

Microsoft, Apple Mac, Linux

These are examples of operating systems – the interface your computer runs. Without an operating system, a blank screen would come up when you turn your computer on. Microsoft is the most popular, Apple Macs are popular with photographers and graphic designers, and Linux is a favourite of 'geeks' because it's open-source, meaning it's free and you can edit the code of the system to customise it.

Broadband

Broadband is a much faster connection to the internet than standard 56k dial-up modem services. Also, it has its own line, so it doesn't tie up a phone line and is permanently connected to the internet. It's relatively cheap these days, at around £14.99 a month for a 1mb connection – theoretically over 18x faster than a 56k dial-up modem.

Photoshop

Photoshop is actually a very expensive program used by professional photographers and image creators to edit digital images and photos. The word 'photoshop' has now become a neologism, meaning to edit an image in some way – 'Oh I'll photoshop out your red eyes.'

eBay

eBay is an online auction site where members can buy and sell their unwanted items. People also use eBay as a marketplace to start a business selling specific goods. Membership is free but you must give a percentage of your takings to eBay.

PayPal

PayPal is a method of paying for goods online. You can create a free account with your debit/credit card details and pay for goods and services where you see the PayPal logo. It offers some security against your purchases, and because it's owned by eBay, it's the most common payment method on eBay. You can also create an account to accept payments via PayPal, so for example if you want to sell goods on eBay and receive PayPal payment. A basic merchant account is free, but if you want to receive payments, you have to pay an extortionate percentage of your takings to PayPal.

Communication

MSN, AOL, Y! IM

These are all examples of Instant Messaging (IM) programs. Teenagers create an account and choose which friends to add or block on their contact list. We then 'chat' to our friends by writing, as the name suggests, free instant messages. It's like a private chat room or extended text messaging, and most teens are signed into their IM accounts chatting to friends whilst multitasking on the computer, browsing websites and listening to music as well.

Forums

Simply, forums are online communities. They're public message boards where a member will start a topic, e.g. 'What is your favourite band?' and other members post a reply. These differ from chat rooms as they're more formal, and posts are saved on the internet forever. You need to register a free account on most forums. Forums can be found about every subject imaginable – from Music to Maths, Guitars to George Michael.

Chatrooms

Chatrooms are like big, public MSN conversations. Unlike forums, the messages aren't archived on the internet forever. Again, like MSN, chatrooms are real-time conversations between people sitting behind their computers all over the world. Lots of people use chatrooms as a way of creating a new identity for themselves; some have ulterior motives, some do it just for fun. Like forums, chatrooms are free to use, and you can find one about every subject imaginable.

VoIP

Stands for Voice over IP, technology used to make phone calls via the internet to people all round the world. You don't have to pay a penny for phone calls to other computers. You need to download a program like SKYPE or MSN to provide an interface for using this technology.

SMS

SMS stands for Short Message Service, aka text messages. Text messaging is much preferred by teenagers over making phone calls, as they're sometimes more convenient, fun, and its easier to say certain things (like 'You're dumped') via text. Texts normally cost about 10p per message, no matter how many characters are used (although there's a limit of 160 characters a message).

Blog

A blog is simply an online diary on a webpage. You can create a free account on a blog website, log in, then update your blog whenever you like. "Blog" is the noun, "to blog" is the verb.

MySpace

MySpace is a social-networking community where users can sign up for their free 'space'. Users' spaces take the form of a blog, user profile, user-uploaded photos, links to their friends' MySpace pages, and the facility to send internal messages to other users. MySpace started in the US and has spread to other countries including the UK, becoming a worldwide phenomenon. It's particularly popular amongst the teenage alternative music community, an easy way for bands and fans to keep in touch. This reputation has backfired a bit, as many people think of MySpace as a no-go area thanks to its domination by 'whiney teen wannabes with no lives'.

Bebo

Bebo is a social-networking website exactly the same as MySpace, except it doesn't have the whiney-teen-wannabe tag – yet.

Chat Abbreviations

WUBU2

Txt/online speak for 'what have you been up to?'

BRB

Meaning 'be right back', commonly said on MSN and in chatrooms where the user has to leave the conversation for a few minutes, e.g. the phone rings. It's acceptable to use "brb" when you're only going to be away for a few minutes; any more, and you should say…

BBS

Meaning 'be back soon'. Used on MSN and in chatrooms if you're going to be away for more than a few minutes, perhaps from 10 – 40 minutes. If you're going to be away but still online for longer than that, you should say…

BBL

Meaning 'be back later'. Used on MSN and in chatrooms if you're going to be away for a while, i.e. over 40 minutes.

BK

"bk" stands for, quite simply, 'back'. It's used whenever a user returns to an MSN conversation or chatroom after saying brb/bbs/bbl.

FFS

Come on, be imaginative – for f's sake!

WTF

Another f word – 'what the f!'

BTW

By the way.

CBA

Can't be arsed.

ATM

At the moment – not automatic teller machine, ye old fogies!

Music

MP3

An "mp3" is actually a type of music file. However, these days, the word "mp3" is commonly used in the following contexts: 'I'm getting an mp3 for my birthday!' and 'I've downloaded 10 mp3s today.' In the first instance, what has been said is actually incorrect; what is meant is 'I am getting an mp3 *player* for my birthday', like an iPod. The second instance is the correct usage of the word "mp3".

iPod

An iPod is a device that plays music. Unlike Walkmans, it doesn't take cassettes or CDs; it has storage – a hard drive – like a computer. You connect the iPod to your computer via a cable and upload the songs on your computer onto the device. Then you plug your headphones into the iPod and listen to your music on the move. The Apple iPod is a specific device, but iPod has become a generic term for a digital Walkman.

Kazaa, Napster, Morpheus, Limewire etc.

Kazaa, Napster and Morpheus are examples of popular peer-to-peer file-sharing programs. What these programs do is provide an interface to a file-sharing network. You open up a file-sharing program of your choice, type in the file name you want to find, and the program will search its network and display other users who are willingly hosting that file. You can then double click the file to download it to your computer. File sharing programs like Kazaa and Napster are most commonly used to download music illegally. However, the programs are not doing anything illegal, it is the users who are sharing and downloading copyrighted material who are breaking the law. You can also use file sharing programs like Kazaa and Napster to download legal and illegal photos, videos, programs, documents, and any other sharable files.

BitTorrent

BitTorrent is another type of network for sharing music and other files. BT uses slightly different technology than networks like Kazaa and Napster, but I won't go into that; all you need to know is that when your teens talk about 'leaving BT running overnight', they're probably downloading a big film or something – legally, of course…

Gaming

MMORPGs

Massively multiplayer online role-playing games, MMORPGs, have become widely talked about in recent years. Users take on the role of a fantasy character and control its actions, interacting in a virtual world with a large number of other users in similar roles. Some games are totally free, others you subscribe to monthly. In some games you can use real currency to buy credits, items and 'land' to use in the game. MMORPGs can be highly addictive as the aim of the game is to train your character up to high levels, moving up the classes within a virtual world. MMORPGs have gained recent press attention as some players spend tens of thousands of real dollars on virtual land.

First Person Shoot-Em-Ups

First Person Shoot-em-ups, FPS's, are games like CounterStrike, Halo, Doom and CallOfDuty. In these games, the player takes a first-person view of the character, with a gun outstretched as if being held by the player. The aim is commonly to save a person, escape a place or to just 'blow the living shite out of everything' (Kevin, FPS player), the player having to achieve objectives as he goes. There are specific FPS's designed for online play, such as CounterStrike, where players connect to servers around the world. Players then compete against other people over the internet.

Other Technology Acronyms

TFT

Stands for thin film transistor. A TFT is a very thin LCD panel commonly used for computer monitors.

P2P

Peer-to-peer – a type of network used with file sharing software like Kazaa and Napster. It literally means the sharing is done from one computer to another – peer to peer. There is no central network where files are hosted.

Music – Playing and Creating

Introduction

Want to have the ultimate respect from your teens? Make them want to be seen with you, and be envied by their peers for doing so?

In this chapter we'll discuss how you can use music to do exactly this. Make your teens think you're cool; and if you're cool, you'll gain their respect – something vital if you want to have a great relationship with them.

Nowadays, the type of music teens listen to depends on the clothes we wear and the friends we keep. Or is it the other way round? I discuss the different types of music relating to different groups, helping parents identify things about their teens just from the sort of noise coming from their bedroom door.

I then talk about the flipside – making music. I explain why I think parents should never force a child to have a music lesson but encourage their natural interests. I talk about my experience of playing the guitar. What's the best way of helping a teen with a natural desire to learn an instrument – find them a teacher, let them teach themselves, enrol on local evening courses? The pros and cons of each and what has worked for me and friends.

I've discovered a new band. Wait, I lie; I've been *recommended* a new band. Oh dear, I've lied again; they're not new.

The KLF, an electrifying rock band, were making themselves known when I was toddling around in nappies reciting Mary Had A Little Lamb.

15 years later, they're at the top of my iTunes playlist and in the CD player in dad's car.

So how did I manage to persuade dad to play electronic rock music in his car? Surely he'd have a fit; something calm and BBC Radio 4ish must be much more up his street. Well, here's the catch: dad was the one that recommended The KLF to me.

Now how cool is that?

I bet it's your ultimate dream to be described as "cool" by your teenagers. And with "cool", respect comes naturally – respect, the number one thing you must gain if you are to have any influence, control or input into/over your child's life from their 13th birthday onwards.

> Kill two birds with one stone: if your teenagers think you're cool, you gain their respect.

Music is something everyone can enjoy, something we discover in our teenage years. Music is a drug, an emotional experience, life changing, inspiring. Teenagers' lives seem to revolve around music: not least their friendship groups are determined by what they listen to. If they're not listening to music they're talking about music, making music, watching MTV, and ruining the paint on their bedroom walls by sticking up posters of their favourite bands.

There's nothing we like more than exchanging mp3s with our friends, recommending each other new bands we've just discovered.

It's such a wonderful feeling when you recommend somebody a song or a new band and they love it just as much as you do; you feel connected through the piece of music, understanding each other's emotions. It's a truly awesome feeling.

…And the best thing? There is nothing stopping parents joining in this practice.

Perhaps your daughter likes Will Young (God help her)? Dig out that Bryan Adams cassette and play it in the car when you next take her somewhere. Don't say anything. Wait for her to start tapping along, singing along, wondering who this latest artist is; then reveal that it is in fact the bloke you had a crush on when you were her age. She might pretend she hates it and turn it off, but look in your cassette player the next day and the tape will have miraculously disappeared.

Alternatively, you might've been a young metal-head back in your day and your son seems to have followed your footsteps. You've never told him about the old times though, so he just thinks you're a totally uncool old fogie who used to disco down to the Village People. Surprise him one day – turn up that Led Zep CD and mosh away, or dust off that BC Rich Flying V guitar and bash out Stairway To Heaven. He'll probably be dead embarrassed at first, telling you how his mates will laugh when they find out his dad's an old rocker, but the next day he'll go to school and tell all of his friends just how cool his dad is. Man, his friends will be so jealous. *So* jealous, I'm telling you. You never know, your son might even invite you to a gig or two!

> Recommend some music to your teenager that you think they may enjoy.

Don't worry about the music you like being decades old. If it's good music, it's good music, and even teenagers can realise that. Well, almost… just don't tell them it's old at first. Let them get into it, then reveal that it's what you were raving to at their age. Boy I'd love to see their expressions.

Equally, there's nothing cooler than me recommending dad some modern music I like and dad turns out to love it – I recently put a Muse album in dad's car, for example, and he quite liked it. He did complain they got a bit dreary after a while, but I just think he's not turning it up loud enough. Good Charlotte and Maroon 5 (I don't care what you purists say… *I* like them) were another two I recommended to dad. He loved them both, and it was often me telling dad to turn it down, not the other way round.

> Listen to some of the music your teen likes – ask them for recommendations.

However, don't just *try* and be cool by buying your teenagers whatever CDs they want instead of really getting involved. It will only make them think you're buying them out of guilt, so are a bit of a pushover: you have to make a real effort, drop your barriers, and immerse yourselves in the music they like.

> Don't just buy your teenagers CDs. Actively involve yourself in the music they listen to.

It's so cool when we're tearing down the M25 playing The KLF, Muse, or any other band really loudly. "Look at that teenager in the car with their dad," I think, "I bet they're not listening to some damn cool rock music. I am. My dad's awesome, he's so, so cool. You're jealous. Envy me and my relationship with my dad!"

I bet you didn't think it was possible that your teenager would want to be seen with you, let alone be envied for doing so. There are a lot of things you don't think possible, but with my amazing book, you'll master it all in no time. Ah yes, got to get a bit of book pimpin' in every now and again ;-)

My point is, don't be shy to recommend some old-school music to your teenager. Retro is all the fad at the moment no matter what 'scene' you're into. Even if your teen's reaction to your closet-music is bad at first, they think you're cool really (well there are probably a few exceptions). I mean come on, could there be *anything* cooler for a teenager than discovering the dad they previously thought was the most uncool person ever secretly likes the same music they like? No. Trust me here, there's not.

So now you've got the urge to recommend some music to your teens, what should you suggest? You know they like rock music, but is it pop-rock indie stuff, or more punk-rock? There's a big difference, and it will pay to get it right.

Well, hopefully you remember the categories we talked about earlier in the fashion chapter: chavs, goths, emos, skaters etc. With any luck you've identified which category your teen belongs to. Have a quick look back at the "Fashion" chapter to refresh your memory. A major part of belonging to one of those fashion groups is to listen to a certain type of music.

This gives you lot another way to identify which group your teen fits in, and vice versa – you can find out what music they like by looking in their wardrobe. Of course there will always be exceptions, but the majority of chavs, for example, will like rap/hip-hop/R'n'B etc. It's unlikely they'd like heavy metal, but everyone has their differences.

Here's a table of the groups we covered in the Fashion chapter, and the music they're most likely to be into:

Group	Genre of music	Example bands	Possible crossovers
Emo	Emotional pop-punk/rock	My Chemical Romance, Taking Back Sunday, Fall Out Boy and Dashboard Confessional	Indie rock, e.g. Kaiser Chiefs, Arctic Monkeys, Franz Ferdinand
Goth	Metal/heavy metal	Marilyn Manson, Nightwish, Dragonforce	Classic rock, e.g. AC/DC, Guns 'n Roses, Pink Floyd
Chav	R'n'B/Rap/Hip-hop/ D'n'B	Eminem, The Streets, D12, Nelly, 50 Cent	Dance, e.g. DJ Tiesto, Scooter, Ian Van Dahl.
Grunger	Heavy rock, 'screamo'	System of a Down, Rage Against The Machine, Nirvana, Slipknot	Classic rock, e.g. Guns 'n Roses, AC/DC, Pink Floyd.
Skater	Indie rock/punk rock	Rage Against The Machine, The Offspring, Rage Against The Green Day, Rancid, Bad Religion	Classic rock, e.g. AC/DC, Guns 'n Roses, Pink Floyd etc.

Surfer	Surf rock (e.g. The Beach Boys), modern rock (e.g. Jack Johnson)	The Beach Boys, Jack Johnson	Classic rock, e.g. AC/DC, Guns 'n Roses, Pink Floyd, Jimi Hendrix etc.
Hippy	Reggae, old rock, trip-hop, jungle/ D'n'B	Bob Marley, The Beatles, Jimi Hendrix, Massive Attack, Aphrodite	Classic rock, e.g. AC/DC, Guns 'n Roses, Pink Floyd etc.
Fashionistas	Indie rock, charts	Kaiser Chiefs, Arctic Monkeys	
Normal	Charts, pop	Gnarls Barkley, Coldplay, Kooks, Kaiser Chiefs, Katie Melua, Red Hot Chili Peppers	Dance, e.g. DJ Tiesto, Scooter, Ian Van Dahl

So we have now thoroughly exhausted the subject of listening to music, but what about the flipside: *making* music?

I'm sure you will agree, learning an instrument is a great thing for teenagers to do. It focuses our attention on something constructive, and learning an instrument takes a lot of self-discipline.

Sometimes, you won't have a problem encouraging your teen to pick up an instrument. They might already have the desire to thrash out those power chords like Slash, or do a Chris Martin (Coldplay) on the piano. However, you still need to decide how best to go about filling their enthusiasm. Do you buy them a guitar and let them get on with it themselves? How about lessons? Are there any cheaper options?

Putting aside the simple option of playing with friends, I've tried and tested a lot of these methods myself with my instrument of choice, the guitar. I've taught myself, had lessons, attended an expensive part-time music academy, and gone along to free jamming sessions with local musicians. They've all had their ups and downs, with some standing out as better than others, so I'll give you a low-down on what each approach entails.

Teaching Yourself

It's so easy to teach yourself an instrument these days, with the help of the internet, friends, books and magazines. There are many free internet forums, chatrooms and websites dedicated to individual instruments catering from the absolute beginner to the professional. Online lessons are plentiful, ranging from the basics of plugging a guitar in, to working out the relative minor of a C7maj.

However, teaching yourself takes a lot of dedication and self-discipline. With nobody there to answer to – 'You haven't done your practice this week' – you have to be extremely self-motivated and dedicated for this method to work. It can be very hard at times when you get stuck, and a picture or paragraph of text on a website just isn't an adequate explanation.

> Pros: Resources are free and plentiful. You don't have to leave your home or pay anyone for lessons.
>
> Cons: Takes an enormous amount of self-discipline. Can be very hard to start with. Nobody to explain something face-to-face. Not motivated/inspired by another person playing with you. Don't develop skills of playing with other musicians.

Private Tutor/Lessons

Private lessons have none of the disadvantages of teaching yourself; there is a tutor there to answer to, you can ask as many questions as you like, you can be shown how to play something in real life, the tutor's playing can inspire you, and you develop skills of playing with another musician.

Of course, lessons cost a lot, and you often have to book them weeks in advance with popular tutors. You will still need self-discipline to practise during the week and do homework.

If the tutor isn't very good, this may lead to a lack of motivation, and music lessons will become just as tedious as your teen's worst lesson at school. Some tutors follow recognised curricula and work on the basis that their students will take exams. Curricula like this don't give budding musicians an individually tailored approach, and exams can put teens off from playing/practising/learning.

Pros: 1-to-1 attention to ask questions. Real-life explanations, e.g. where to put your fingers. Real-life inspiration. Develop skills playing with another musician.

Cons: Cost a lot. Might have to book in advance. May have to go to tutor's house. An un-inspirational tutor is detrimental to your teen's learning. Curricula aren't individually tailored to your teen's needs. Exams put teens off.

Part-Time Music Courses

Lots of music academies and local colleges offer part-time music courses, running once a week for an hour or so. Courses vary; some are simply like school classes, with teachers teaching a group of 20 or so students who don't interact with each other much.

There are other courses designed to get the students playing together, where students are given a song to learn over the week then come back the next week and play it together. These types of courses aren't designed to teach you much; the idea is to have fun playing with other musicians and to learn basic 'band skills'.

These courses can be very expensive, and you rarely get 1-to-1 attention from a teacher, despite being run by professional musicians.

> Pros: Exciting to go along to a college/academy. Good way of meeting other musicians. Fun and educational playing with other musicians.
>
> Cons: Very expensive, not 1-to-1 attention, don't learn much musically speaking.

Local Free Jamming Sessions

Local jamming sessions are an excellent way of learning an instrument and playing with other musicians – best of all, they're free. Sessions like this are often organised by the local council or other associations, such as youth groups, schools and music shops. These sorts of groups are led by professional musicians, and can have up to 20 or 30 participants.

Unlike some of the expensive part-time courses above, the focus of these groups is to get together in bands and write your own songs. This encourages proper song-writing skills that will stretch your musical knowledge, and of course you're in a real band situation. Because the professional musicians on hand to help are normally volunteers, they tend to give you more attention and 1-to-1 help.

The skill range in these groups varies widely, which is good if you're a beginner; having better players around you inspires you to learn your instrument. Depending on the location of the event (e.g. at a school), you can sometimes borrow instruments for free.

Downsides of this approach are: having to travel to the venue, and having to fit in a band – my experience has been that the locations where older teenagers go (14+) are often full, so I have to go to the less popular places with younger teenagers (11–13) and they're less mature about wanting to play and learn their instrument seriously.

Pros: Free. 1-to-1 attention from professional musicians. Learn song-writing skills. Learn to work in a band. Good for beginners to be round better players. Borrow instruments for free.

Cons: Have to travel to the venue. Groups with older teenagers tend to be full.

So now you have the facts, weigh up the pros and cons, and decide which option would work best for you and your teenager. I would recommend combining a couple of them for the best results – a private tutor and free local jamming sessions might work well together, for instance.

Whatever you do, don't force your teenager to play an instrument. You may think it's best for them – and sure, it would be great if we all learnt instruments – but if your teen doesn't have the desire, motivation, and inspiration to learn, you will be wasting your time and money and are likely to do more damage than good.

An example: my dad's parents used to make him – well, they *encouraged* him – to have piano lessons as a young boy. He absolutely hated it, his teacher sucked, he wasn't inspired to be a great player, and he had to do hours of monotonous practice. The result? He quit as soon as he could and vowed never to touch a musical instrument again. Well… he hasn't quite stuck to his word. Dad has recently taken up the piano and is teaching himself, after being inspired to play by blues pianist Jools Holland. However, because he's left it so late – remember, he was put off instruments for 20 or so years – he isn't able to remember lots of the theory needed to be able to make the next step from competent Fur Elise player to an improvisational blues player. It does make you wonder: if dad didn't have those hated piano lessons as a boy, he wouldn't have been put off playing an instrument. If that was the case, he might have been inspired to play the piano a lot earlier, and could have been the new Jools Holland…

> Don't force your teens to learn an instrument.

Homework:

○ Ask your teen to recommend some of their music for you to listen to.

○ Recommend some of your favourite 'oldies' music that your teen might enjoy.

○ Choose an old tape of yours that you think your teen might like and put it on in the car when you next give your teen a lift somewhere. Be subtle, be patient, and just wait for their reaction...

○ Ask your teen if they would like to learn an instrument, and support them in doing so using whichever method they choose – advise them of the pros and cons of each.

Tell Me Where You're Going

Introduction

I decided to include this chapter in How Teenagers Think because I know from experience that a lot of parents have trouble getting their teens to tell them their whereabouts. At least, if you're anything like my parents, it would be fair to assume that you like to nag your teenagers about where they're going. And, if your teenagers are anything like me, the reply you are likely to get is a slammed door. Therefore, I'm taking an educated guess that you might like some help with getting your teens to tell you where they're going.

I interview a friend about why they don't tell their parents where they're going, but also see how parents are at fault as well.

Kev came round t'other day. He arrived at the train station here at about 1pm, and we dropped him back off at the station at about 10pm. His journey home entailed an hour's train ride, a short ferry trip across a river, and a 15-minute cycle home through some dodgy areas at 11.30 at night. Nice.

Of course, he hadn't told his parents he'd be out that day. Well, they'd guessed he was out – but they didn't know where he was. They didn't know he had been 35 odd miles away at 10pm.

Well, that's awful, you must be thinking. Does Kev not care for his safety? Surely we know that it's safest for us if we tell our parents at least where we're going to be and when we're getting back? After all, we don't want to be murdered or abducted any more than you want us to.

True. I agree. It seems silly that Kev didn't tell his parents. But don't you think we're being a bit rude, talking about Kev behind his back? Yeah, I think so. OK then, let's ask Kev what he thinks…

> **jellyellie:** So Kev, you came up to see me the other day, didn't you?
>
> **Kev:** Maybe. Yes, yes I did. And my parents were 100% unaware of it.
>
> **jellyellie:** Why didn't you tell them?
>
> **Kev:** Partly because there was no one in to tell, but mainly because I never do.
>
> **jellyellie:** OK, but don't you think it would be safer for you if you told them? So, telling them would benefit you?
>
> **Kev:** Yeah. It would. It's just something I've NEVER done before.
>
> **jellyellie:** OK, I see. Would you feel silly telling them, breaking the habit?
>
> **Kev:** Yeah. Sommat like that.
>
> **jellyellie:** What about knowing that you could stop them from worrying about where you are by telling them?

Kev: I guess I feel bad about not actually telling them. I sometimes tell them, but only if they're not going to whinge.

jellyellie: A-hah! There is a gem of insider's knowledge there. So if you think they might whinge about where you're going, you won't tell them?

Kev: Yeah. If I'm going out drinking or whatever I'll tell them though I suppose, because they won't whinge and if I'm going to come back drunk it's sometimes nice to let them know. But normally I'm drinking round here with people anyway so, blah.

jellyellie: OK, that's nice of you – I bet there are tonnes of teens out there who wouldn't be so considerate!

Kev: Hehehe. If I go to your party I'll tell them I'm going to a party, I just won't tell them it's in ******* [jellyellie's town, blanked for the stalkers].

jellyellie: Wait a sec. IF you come to my party? Don't you mean when you come to my party???

Kev: Hahah. Yeah.

jellyellie: Ya better.

Well, that was quite interesting. Let's summarise Kev's main points:

○ He doesn't tell his parents where he's going because:
   – There's nobody around to tell.
   – It's not a habit he has got into.

○ Kev knows it would be safer for him to tell his parents where he is, but after not doing this for a few years, he would feel almost babyish suddenly keeping them informed of his whereabouts.

○ Knowing that his parents are worrying about where he is does bother Kev a bit, but not enough to make him tell his parents where he is.

Kev does tell his parents where he's going but only when he knows they won't complain.

So although Kev's situation may be a little unusual in the fact that his parents don't seem to mind about where he is, the solution to get him to tell his parents of his whereabouts is exactly the same as the solution to get a teenager whose parents do want to know where they are – and the key lies in the last point, "Kev does tell his parents where he's going but only when he knows they won't complain". The principle is similar to what we talked about in the Internet chapter – if your teens know you'll be angry, they just won't bother telling you, so they'll be even less safe.

Perhaps your teenagers haven't been telling you where they're going because they're worried you would get angry and stop them from going? This could very well be a contributing factor to their attitude.

> Lots of teens don't tell their parents where they're going because they're worried they'll be angry.

Instead of sitting around worrying when your teenagers will come home, you can take a proactive role. Let your teenagers know that you won't flip out if they say they're going to a gig, or a party, or wherever else you don't want them going. Let them know that you'd prefer them to tell you they're going someplace like that rather than not tell you at all because they're scared you'll be angry.

Of course, after committing yourself to that, you need to hold back the anger when they do tell you they're going somewhere you don't approve of. Remember that 'be consistent' thing? This is a prime example. If you say you won't be angry but you then get angry, your teens will lose all trust and respect for you. Back to the starting line, my friend.

So if the situation occurs where your teen is telling you she's going to an opium den in India with a 23-year old she met off the internet, forget the anger, you should be thankful that she has told you. She obviously has respect for you – she wants to stop you from worrying, and she respects that you will keep your word and not flip out.

> Let your teens know that you won't be angry if they tell you where they're going and you don't approve. Keep to your word.

Now, let's go back to Kev…

jellyellie: So Kev, we've talked about how you might be at fault here – not telling your parents where you're going. But what do you think they could do to encourage you to tell them?

Kev: Maybe ask me.

jellyellie: What, they don't ask you where you're going?

Kev: Sometimes. They generally don't.

jellyellie: Isn't that cool, though, the freedom?

Kev: Yeah I f'ing love it. I think maybe they trust me in that respect, and don't treat me like a child still. Because to be fair, I'm 17 next month so I could learn to drive and go anywhere or whatever.

So Kev loves the fact that his parents don't bother to ask where he's going…

> Teens like it when their parents don't check up on them…

Kev: It's kinda annoying that they won't phone me, or anything, though. They probably don't do it because I just tell them to stop worrying if they do. So yeah I guess that's why they don't check up on me.

Ah, but what is Kev saying now? He *does* want his parents to check on him? But then when they do ask where he is… he'll moan at them? What! How confusing and hypocritical!

> …but teens also feel insecure when their parents don't check up on them.

Actually – and as much as he will hate me for saying this – Kev is a very typical teenager in that sense; confusing and hypocritical. You can't blame us though – we have just been granted teen independence, yet we are still learning how to deal with our emotions, and we're still forming our own opinions and values. Therefore we often take hypocritical stances; sometimes by accident, sometimes to try out different thoughts and ideas. So don't be hard on your teens – one day they may relish the freedom you give them, other days they may want a phone call from you so they know you still care about them, and it's perfectly normal.

> Don't argue with your teens if they seem to relish your attention one day and refuse to tell you where they are the next. We're just growing up.

In conclusion, then, I think it's fair to say that while we are enjoying our freedom, we're still children, so appreciate a call or a text every now and again to feel secure in the knowledge you still love us. Actually, yes, texts are a great idea – no embarrassing "Yes, mum, I'm with my mates... yes... mum!!! Stop worrying about me!!!" type calls; texts have less scope for arguments; and hey, if parents can text, they're seriously cool.

> Send your teens a text every now and again to make sure they're OK.

Homework

○ Let your teens know that you won't be angry when they say they're going to places you might not approve of, and you would prefer them to tell you than not tell you and go anyway. Keep this promise.

○ Don't argue with your teens if one minute they're moaning at you for keeping checking up on them, but the next they ask why you don't call them as it makes them feel unloved.

○ Send your teen the occasional text when they're out and about to make sure they're OK.

Siblings

Introduction

I let you in on what it's like to be a teenager with a sibling, younger or older, and what you should do when it comes to sibling squabbles.

Chapter Dedication

Seeing as this chapter is about siblings, I thought it would be a nice idea if I dedicated it to my own smelly brother. And I promised him I would include this:

> **Alex:** Am I in it [my book]?
>
> **jellyellie:** Umm, yeah.
>
> **Alex:** How much?
>
> **jellyellie:** Not much really.
>
> **Alex:** Why not? I want to be in it!
>
> **jellyellie:** OK cool, I'll interview you then.
>
> **Alex:** No! I refuse to be interviewed.
>
> **jellyellie:** Right.
>
> **Alex:** Yeah put that actually, that I refuse to comment.

Here's to you, Alex.

As I am writing this, my brother is punching me in the arm. It hurts; he's a lot bigger than me, despite being 16 months younger. I just heard dad shout something incoherent at us, and Alex and I haven't stopped arguing since, so that means dad will probably come bursting in any second now. His most likely course of action will be to send us to our rooms. I'll grab my book on the way up and, still swearing at my brother (is he really related to me?), slam my bedroom door behind me as hard as I can.

Anyway, it's all a bit petty really. We're arguing for no reason – just something I said annoyed Alex, then his reply annoyed me, and my reply annoyed him etc... I'm sure I will look back on this in a few years time and cringe.

I don't know why we argue. In fact, that says it all – there never is a real reason. It starts over one small thing and just continues to escalate until we end up whacking each other with cushions, then our fists.

> The majority of sibling feuds have no real basis... it's all just a bit of petty squabbling for the sake of it when tempers rise.

The most annoying thing, however, is when parents step in. They always take sides, which immediately escalates the problem even further by antagonising one child, and they tend to blow the whole thing out of proportion when we could have calmed down by ourselves after a while.

I will go on to explain further why I think it's best for parents to leave us to sort out our disputes, but for now, I think the best way to continue with this chapter is to talk to some teenagers and see how they all feel about their relationships with their siblings. First of all let's talk to Kev, who's 17, and has a younger brother Ryan, who's 12.

We spoke to Kev in the "Stop Treating Me Like A Child" chapter, where he complained that he was treated unfairly in comparison to his younger brother Ryan. Does this make him loathe his brother? Let's find out how the pair get on, and this time, we'll hear from Ryan as well…

Interview with Ryan

jellyellie: How old are you?

Ryan: 12, I'm a boy.

jellyellie: How old is your sibling?

Ryan: 17, he's a boy – Kev.

jellyellie: Do you spend a lot of time with Kev?

Ryan: Not quite an hour a day.

jellyellie: Do you have many common interests?

Ryan: No!

jellyellie: Do you respect Kev/look up to him?

Ryan: Not really.

jellyellie: Do you think Kev respects you? Would you like him to respect you?

Ryan: I don't think he does respect me and I wouldn't really care if he did or didn't.

jellyellie: Be honest – do you like to hang around Kev in public, or in front of his/your friends to look cool?

Ryan: No.

jellyellie: How well do you get on with Kev?

Ryan: Fairly well.

jellyellie: Did you used to get on with Kev a lot better when you were both younger or do you feel your relationship has improved/worsened as Kev has grown up?

Ryan: I used to hate him when we were younger, so it's a lot better now he's older. I don't really know why I hated him; he was just so annoying.

jellyellie: Do you argue a lot with Kev?

Ryan: I used to, but we don't much now.

jellyellie: What do you argue about?

Ryan: I can't really remember! I guess that means just silly pointless things.

jellyellie: How do your parents deal with the situation when you argue?

Ryan: Most of the time they aren't in, and that's when we argue – when they're in, we don't argue, but if we do, they tell us off badly.

jellyellie: Is there anything you would like your parents to do differently with you Ryan, e.g. leave you to sort arguments out, treat you like your older sibling etc?

Ryan: No – come on, let me go now, I want to play my new Gameboy game!!

Now let's see what Kev has to say…

Interview with Kev

jellyellie: How old is your sibling?

Kev: 12 today! Little Ryan.

jellyellie: Do you spend a lot of time with Ryan?

Kev: Maybe an hour a day. I try and influence him with my (awesome might I add) taste in music, or just talk and stuff. Lately I've gone outside in the garden with my guitar too when he's been out there (and the neighbours even recognised something I was playing! yeaah)!

jellyellie: Do you have many common interests?

Kev: Err, nope.

jellyellie: Do you respect Ryan?

Kev: As much as I hate to say it, yeah! I'm not sure why I respect him though – I guess I've always had respect for younger people. I'm not an egotistical jerk even though lots of people think I am. Spending time with people older than me at college has made me respect younger people more too.

jellyellie: Do you think Ryan respects you? Would you like him to respect you?

Kev: I think he probably does, he just doesn't want to admit it – at least I hope he does :-)

jellyellie: Do you think it's annoying when Ryan hangs around you in public, or in front of his/your friends trying to be cool?

Kev: Not really, well the other day he was trying to be helpful when my friends where round and it pissed me off and I told him to f off. I dunno, it felt like he was trying to be 'cool' in front of my friends. Like he wouldn't go away when everyone was gonna light up. Otherwise no, we played football against some chavs with him the other day, one of the fat lairy dicks was being lairy to him and I really wanted to punch the shite (got my own back though by running and jumping into the f'er and tackling him hard against the fence).

jellyellie: How well do you get on with Ryan?

Kev: Err, an awful lot better than I used to that's for sure! We used to argue nearly every day about stupid things.

jellyellie: Did you used to get on with Ryan a lot better when you were both younger or do you feel your relationship has improved as you have matured? Or do you get on worse now because you're mature and he's not?

Kev: Definitely improved as I've grown the f' up this last year.

jellyellie: Do you argue a lot with Ryan?

Kev: Not as much as we used to, but occasionally.

jellyellie: What do you argue about?

Kev: Stupid pointless shit.

jellyellie: How do your parents deal with the situation when you argue?

Kev: They aren't normally in – if they are, they tell me to grow up.

jellyellie: Is there anything you would like your parents to do differently with you and your sibling? e.g. leave you to sort arguments out, treat you like your younger sibling etc.

Kev: Err, I guess maybe treat us equally.

So there we go ladies and gentlemen, true brotherly love! Now then, let's pick those interviews apart and see what we can find out...

One of the few things Ryan & Kev actually agreed on was the fact that they don't have anything in common. I'm sure neither of them is exaggerating; I would similarly struggle to name one thing I have in common with my brother. Wait I thought of one – we can kick a football around together. OK, so I would struggle to think of two things I have in common with my brother.

When I asked a wider range of teenagers if they had many things in common with their siblings, the answer was pretty much unanimous, bar the odd few who seem to be very lucky and have a long string of similar interests. At a stretch, most of my friends managed to think of perhaps one or two things – same kind of humour, same music, but that's pretty much it. In fact, **Josh, 15,** summed it up perfectly:

"Erm... we share the same parents... and house."

So really, for the majority of teenagers, they don't have much in common with their siblings; and it's pretty likely that were they not related, they wouldn't choose to be friends in a million years. But still we manage to get along, so parents, give us a bit of credit.

> It's normal for siblings to have few things of common interest.

Now then, back to Kev and Ryan...

Despite agreeing that they have nothing in common, Kev & Ryan both went on to say that they get on fairly well.

> This is important to note – just because siblings don't have many common interests, this doesn't mean that we can't get on well.

Kev and Ryan also reported that their relationship has definitely improved in the past year or so as Kev, the oldest, has grown up.

It's funny, because I know a few other siblings who say the opposite thing – as one of them has matured, they fight even more, as the mature sibling makes their own way in the world and the younger sibling still remains comparatively immature. Then, when the younger child becomes mature, they become closer and get on a lot better.

> Siblings' relationships change when the eldest one reaches maturity. The relationship may change for the better or worse, but, if it's for the worse, as the younger sibling catches up, the relationship normally improves again.

Therefore, it's probably hard to guess what will happen to the relationship between your children when your oldest sibling reaches maturity in their teenage years. It's not important what happens, however, as there's nothing you can do about this. What is important is to let your kids squabble and fight, then sort matters out by themselves; it's beneficial if we have our own space to do this, not least because we are bound to have to work out differences with others in the future, but it's also great character building.

> Let your kids fight and leave it to them to sort out their differences.

Homework

○ Let your teenagers squabble between themselves; don't break them up, or take sides.

Peer Pressure

Introduction

I discuss what makes teenagers particularly susceptible to give in to pressure from their peers. A topic that every teenager can relate to, I interview a couple of friends about their experiences with peer pressure.

If I stick '"peer pressure" + teenager' into Google, 2,830,000 results are returned in 0.5 seconds. A quick browse through the links, and the majority are health websites advising parents on how to stop their children succumbing to peer pressure and partaking in underage sex, drinking, drug taking and other forms of 'delinquent' behaviour.

There was the odd good article with advice for teenagers rather than parents, but most of the above articles aimed at parents were pretty naff and based around a few similar principles:

○ Peer pressure is bad.

○ Teenagers succumb to peer pressure.

○ Parents should tell their teenagers peer pressure is bad and that they should avoid being sucked into it.

Now, as Catherine Tate puts it so perfectly, *whaaaaaaaaaat a load of old shit!*

OK parents, listen, a few points to make:

1 If you follow those articles and constantly remind your kids how bad peer pressure is and tell them not to give in to it, you're on the right path to throw away any respect they might have for you.

2 Peer pressure can be good.

3 Although there is a certain type of teenager most likely to succumb to the bulk of peer pressure, at the end of the day it does affect everyone, and continues throughout our whole lives.

Right then, I'd better explain…

1 If you follow those articles and constantly remind your kids how bad peer pressure is and tell them not to give in to it, you're on the right path to throw away any respect they might have for you.

When I did that Google search earlier, I came across an article in response to a question a teenager had emailed in – she said that if her parents told her to not give into peer pressure one more time, she'd scream. Fair enough – I think I'd scream too if my parents kept nagging at me. It's not like we don't know what peer pressure is; we're fully aware of it, and know we should avoid bad peer pressure.

When I finish writing this chapter, I'm going to a friend's house with a group of mates. If my parents say to me "remember, don't be pressurised into doing anything you don't want to" or tell me to "watch out for peer pressure", I think I will go bananas and slam the door very hard on the way out. However, if they maybe *asked* me about how peer pressure affects me, sure, I'd get a bit annoyed upon hearing 'peer pressure', but I realise that instead of thrusting "don't be swayed by peer pressure, stick to your values" down my throat, my parents actually care and they want to understand a bit more about what goes on in my life, and what my relationships are like with my friends. It makes me more likely to respond to them.

> Instead of telling your children to avoid peer pressure, ask them about their experiences with it. Discuss it with them. Small changes like that – something as simple as asking instead of telling – can have the biggest o–f effects.

When doing my research on the internet, I also came across a teenager who had written in to ask a psychologist if all peer pressure is bad or if there is actually such a thing as good peer pressure. Well, what do you think? I bet you're thinking, "Of course not, don't be so ridiculous – peer pressure is bad". Or you now might be thinking the opposite as you realise I am about to say that there is good peer pressure too…

2 Peer pressure can be good.

When we hear the words 'peer pressure', we automatically think of teenagers, and drink, drugs, promiscuous sex and other bad things. So really, we think of peer pressure as a bad thing.

In fact, there are two types of peer pressure. There's bad peer pressure, and good peer pressure, and every person is likely to be affected by both types at some point in their lives.

We all know what bad peer pressure is like. **Emily, 17,** will give us an example:

> "OK. I've always been really against smoking – it stinks, and I hate it when my mates smoke. I've slagged off so many of them for doing it. So the other night, I was at this party, sitting on a bench playing my guitar – slightly drunk (*how* drunk can be left to your imagination, you've seen me drunk, not pretty). Anyway, my friends were smoking (grr) and somehow, in my drunkenness, they shoved a rollie in my mouth, which I happily smoked. Then I really did turn into a hypocrite – later when my friend had another fag I asked him for one. I happily smoked that too, and felt pretty darn cool. I wouldn't consider myself to be the sort of person that'd do something like that just to 'look cool', but I guess I'm wrong."

So that's a pretty familiar story, but can you think of an example of good peer pressure? **Josie, 17,** told me how she was once in a group that stood up to a bully:

> "Me and some mates were walking through a park when we saw this guy we knew from school, Ash, intimidating this little kid who was by himself. We all saw what was going on, and because there were five or six of us and just one bully, we felt pretty confident about going up to him and telling him to leave the kid alone. So that's just what we did, and it worked – Ash left this kid alone. However, if any of us had been walking through that park by ourselves, I doubt we would have done anything. It was being part of a group that influenced us and put pressure on us to go and do something good."

Therefore, peer pressure can be a way for our friends to have a positive influence on us. In fact, because we teens are more heavily influenced by our peers than we are by our parents, it's really important that we do experience positive peer pressure from our friends. This gives us good values to look up to, which are vital as we try and find our identity and role in life.

> Peer pressure isn't always bad. Good peer pressure is an important way for teenagers to adopt good values from their friends and to learn to follow social norms.

Good peer pressure is also necessary to teach us how to follow social norms and how to follow a good crowd, and helps us develop socially. These are all skills that we will need for the rest of our lives – as I go on to talk about next, even adults are affected by peer pressure.

3 Although there is a certain type of teenager most likely to succumb to the bulk of peer pressure, at the end of the day it does affect everyone, and continues throughout our whole lives.

Now then, let's actually talk about bad peer pressure, how it affects teenagers, and what you can do to help your teens.

Firstly, there *are* types of teenagers who will naturally be more susceptible to any type of peer pressure than other teenagers. Teenagers who are generally more reserved, have low self-confidence and low self-esteem, and don't have many strong views of their own are most likely to succumb to peer pressure. This is only natural; because they are perhaps less sure of themselves, they are likely to find it harder to say 'no' when confronted with bad peer pressure, and are likely to want to experiment with things more until they find their values; things that bad peer pressure is likely to offer them.

> Lack of self-confidence and self-esteem is, I believe, the main thing that pushes teenagers to give in to bad peer pressure.

If you think this sounds like your teen, don't worry. Like I said, it's perfectly natural for them to experience peer pressure and perhaps make a few mistakes, and it won't last forever – psychologists generally reckon that by the our late teens we have gone through our 'period of conflict' with the world and have discovered our true identities. But this probably isn't much of a comfort to you at the moment. So, what can you do to help your teenager in the meantime?

The first thing you can do is remember points 1 and 2: don't nag your teens about peer pressure, but discuss the subject with them and make sure that they're aware of the differences between good and bad peer pressure. Try and do this as early as you can, even from seven or eight years old – the younger we are, the less sure we are of our values, so the more open we are to peer pressure.

Secondly, you should concentrate on the direct source of the issue, not the outcome. In this case, the lack of self-confidence is the issue, and the giving-in-to-peer-pressure is the outcome. Here are some ideas to help you improve your teen's self-confidence:

○ Encourage your teenager to place him/herself in situations she's not naturally comfortable with. E.g. ask them to phone up and book their next dentist appointment, or a table in the restaurant. Start small and build their way up.

○ Help boost your teen's self-esteem by praising them for all the little things they do well. Praise their schoolwork, their hobbies, achievements in sports, and anything else they excel in.

○ Encourage your teen to voice their opinions. Ask for their opinions on a news item involving their favourite sport, for example. This gets them building up their self-values and self-confidence.

> If you are aware that your teenagers are susceptible to bad peer pressure, try and build their self-confidence by encouraging them to put themselves into new situations, and their self-esteem by giving them plenty of praise.

So now you have built up confident teens. Awesome! You have protected your children from peer pressure for the rest of their lives.

Or so you thought…

Peer pressure actually continues throughout the whole of our lives. Of course, it changes its form as we grow up – I can't quite imagine the 80 year olds in the care home down the road daring each other to drink shots of absinthe.

Instead, adults are likely to encounter forms of peer pressure that make sure they comply with social norms. For example, would you walk to the shops in the morning in your pyjamas? Walk round the shopping centre with no shoes on in the summer? Of course not! To do so would be to break the social rules of our society, something heavily frowned upon. You may believe that you refrain from doing these activities because it would be 'silly' to go out in your pyjamas, or you actually prefer to wear shoes, but it is peer pressure that makes sure we conform with these social rules of our society.

Peer pressure affects people throughout their whole lives, making sure we conform to healthy social rules.

Homework

○ Discuss peer pressure with your teenagers. Try not to use that phrase though – instead, ask them how they think their friends' values influence their own.

○ Perhaps tell your teens a funny story about something you did when you were younger just because your friends told you to. Stories like these remind us that you were a teenager too, so you do actually know what you're talking about.

Holiday With a Friend

Introduction

So, what happens when your teen refuses to go on holiday with you anymore? Well, that's easy – you bribe them by allowing them to bring a friend (I'll show you how).

Ok, so all of a sudden you're in a foreign country with your family and someone else's teenager. Now what happens? Are you going to let them go off by themselves? Drink alcohol? The responsibility of someone else's child! Sit down, take a deep breath. Have a cup of tea. We'll talk to some teens who have been there, done that, and know how it works.

So you happen to be one of these rare, organised creatures. You booked the annual family holiday the previous October. Your teen was just a mere 14, still getting to grips with the role of being a teenager, and quite looking forward to going away again next summer.

It's now 'next summer', two weeks before you're due to go to Spain. That's not important. Well, it is, but the matter of prime importance is the fact that your teenager is now 15, and well into their period of conflict. They've just dropped a bombshell: "Mum, I'm not going on holiday with you!"

"What? You're what, Maddie?"

"I'm not going on holiday with you! Are you deaf or something?? I'm not going! There's no way you can make me go. There is just no way I'm going to be seen getting on an aeroplane with you and consigning myself to two weeks of absolute boredom, with you, my bloody parents. What a waste of my summer holidays! I'm not going!"

"Maddie! Keep your voice down – all the neighbours can hear!"

"I don't CARE! I'LL SHOUT IF I HAVE TO – I'M NOT GOING!"

"You don't have a choice – we booked and paid for your ticket *months* ago! Don't be such an ungrateful so-and-so! Six months ago you couldn't wait to go."

"Shut up, I'm not going! It's so bloody boring there with you! There is NO WAY I am going, there is NO WAY you can make me go."

"Madeline, stop being ridiculous. You are going whether you like it or not."

"I'm not going. There's no way you can make me go. And don't call me Madeline. I'm not going."

"Take a friend with you or something then! Jess? What about Tammy?"

"Yeah OK. Thanks mum. By the way I'll need a couple of new tops and a bikini then."

"Eh… what? Maddie…?"

Don't you just **love** having teenagers? I hope you do.

So yeah. Your teenager has convinced you to allow him/her to take a friend with them on holiday. Well – they haven't really convinced you. You just sort of offered, and… anyway, that's beside the point.

> If your teen refuses to come on holiday with you, a good idea is to suggest they bring a friend with them. As long as they believe they will have enough freedom and independence on holiday, they should be happy with this compromise.

What you now need to know is what to expect from this whole new set-up. Will you let them go off by themselves? What about drinking? Are you going to have to be responsible for their friend's money? Sleeping arrangements?

I agree. It's a whole new world. You may have been on holiday with your friends and their families when you were a teen, but come on, that was rather a while ago.

Now then, my two friends Conrad and Iain, both 16, have just come back from a week in Greece. Conrad went with his family and invited his friend Iain along too. Shall we have a word with them about how it all worked out? Yes, I think that would be a good idea.

jellyellie: What sort of holiday did you go on?

Iain: Water based activity.

Conrad: Yeah, it was a Neilson shore-based, water-activities and general relaxation holiday, in Greece.

jellyellie: Did you enjoy it?

Iain: Yep it was amazing.

Conrad: Very much so, it was fantabulous.

jellyellie: Conrad, would you have enjoyed it less without Iain?

Conrad: Definitely, having a friend with me was great, as although the people who were there were fantastic, having someone I knew already made it less daunting.

If your teen would be the only child of their age in your family group (i.e. an only sibling; has older siblings who no longer come on holiday with you; or has much younger siblings) they may not want to go on holiday with you because of a lack of teenage contact. Allowing them to bring a friend is an ideal solution to this.

jellyellie: Iain, did you enjoy going on holiday with a friend and without your parents?

Iain: Yes, it was a totally different experience. With a friend you're more relaxed and friends are people you choose so you get along much better.

Did you hear that? No more sibling rivalry.

jellyellie: How did you work out monetary arrangements such as paying for Iain's share of meals?

Iain: My dad gave Conrad's parents a sum of money to cover meals and contribute towards overall costs, and I took some of my own money, so I was free to buy drinks, souvenirs etc.

Conrad: Yeah, I believe that's correct – though we were happy to pay for it all!

jellyellie: What were your sleeping arrangements?

Iain: We had two rooms, parents in one and us in the other.

You can't expect your teenager and his/her friend to share a room with you. If you want to keep your sanity you wouldn't even want to suggest this – do you know how long we spend in the bathroom?!

jellyellie: Were you allowed to go out during the day/evening by yourselves? How did this arrangement work?

Iain: We were allowed to go wherever we wanted in the resort/hotel complex, but when we went into town we stuck together with Conrad's parents.

Conrad: Yeah, in the resort it wasn't a problem, but in the nearby town we didn't really want to go off by ourselves: the teens from our resort that did go were just going to get pissed, which didn't really appeal to us. Generally though we actually saw my parents very little.

If the area is relatively safe, your teens are comfortable with the idea and stick together in as big a group as possible – perhaps with other teenagers from your resort – it is generally a good idea to let them go to the local town without you so they build on their independence (and you get an evening to yourselves).

jellyellie: Were you allowed to drink?

Iain: Conrad's parents checked with my parents beforehand that if I wanted to buy alcohol they would buy a reasonable amount for me – they wouldn't have let me go nuts and get totally legless each night though. So we could have drunk if we wanted to, but neither of us drank any more than a shot of a homebrewed local spirit that was given to us.

Conrad: Yeah, we were given Raki in a restaurant (a home-brewed Greek spirit) – which the waiter made us try, and actually found OK, although it was *very* fiery. It's now the only alcohol that Iain will drink!

Conrad and Iain were perhaps particularly conservative with their alcohol consumption, so if you think your teens are likely to be different, always check with their parents first and set a limit on holiday as to what they can drink – but do allow them to drink something, as prohibition just increases the appeal factor.

jellyellie: Iain, do you feel you've grown as a person and learnt more about yourself having been away without your family?

Iain: To an extent yes, because I was responsible for myself 99% of the time rather than having someone saying 'this is good' or 'that is bad'. It gave me an extended sense of independence. It also makes me appreciate what my parents did for me when I was younger, but now I feel that I've proven myself to be respon-sible etc, so I would feel crowded if they took lots of control now I'm back.

Iain's answer perfectly sums up the benefits of letting your teen go on holiday with a friend's family. They are likely to become more responsible, independent, and even appreciate you more. Just make sure you're not too smothering when they come back home.

jellyellie: Iain, is there anything you would have liked Conrad's parents to have done differently to make you feel more comfortable/welcome/happy etc.?

Iain: No, his parents were great, I felt as if I was being looked after yet free to do just what I wanted.

jellyellie: Conrad, overall, do you think your parents were happy with how the holiday went?

Conrad: Yes, I think they both really enjoyed it, though my dad wanted there to be more wind!

jellyellie: Ah yeah, the joys of sailing. Almost finished now: Conrad, is there anything you wished your parents could have done differently to make the holiday more enjoyable for you and Iain?

Conrad: Stayed there another week! Seriously though, nothing that I can think of. Oh, er, not let me fall ill halfway through!

jellyellie: And guys, any final comments for parents reading this who are thinking about letting their teen take a friend on holiday with them for the first time, or letting them go off with a friend and their family?

Iain: I'd say let them go, chances are that since they are with a friend they will have the time of their lives and develop this friendship further, as well as developing themselves with more responsibility. They can learn to look after themselves, something they can't do with parents, with the safety net of another set of parents to watch over them if need be.

Conrad: Yeah, and don't worry! Teenagers *can* be sensible, and don't need looking after every 10 minutes. On the other hand, if you do want to spend some time with them, just say!

So there we have it ladies and gentlemen, Conrad and Iain. Massive thanks to them both for providing us with an excellent insight into their holiday. I think they are fine examples of teenagers, who indeed just go to prove that we can actually be sensible.

Homework

I know you too well. Just because we are talking about holidays, don't think I'm going to let you off without any homework this chapter. Parents, eh...

○ If you are currently considering your next family holiday, ask your teen whether they would like to take a friend with them. Be proactive like this so you don't end up with an argument like Maddie just before you're about to set off.

○ Ask your friends who also have teenagers if they've ever taken one of their teen's friends on holiday with them, and find out about the arrangements they came to.

Friends

Introduction

We've had Peer Pressure, Holiday With A Friend, and Parties is up next. It's probably about time I gave the subject of 'friends' a chapter of its own. Well, here it is. What would you like to know?

Let's be boffins and talk about clever stuff for a moment. I'm going to introduce you to a fellow boffin, Ericsson, a psychologist who was heavily influenced by the work of Sigmund Freud. Ericsson was one of the first psychologists to come up with a theory on the social development of adolescents. He is now a world-renowned psychologist, and one of his most famous theories was 'adolescents value their peers more than their parents'.

As a parent of a teenager, however, I'm sure you don't need a psychologist to tell you this. In fact, you may be wondering what on earth you actually need to do to be a psychologist: it just seems like common sense, right? But, let's not go there; what is important to note is, yes, as harsh as it sounds, friends are a lot more important to teenagers than our parents are. If you are in denial, listen to what these teens (and teens-at-heart) have to say:

"Do I value my friends over my parents? Yup. I don't think anyone's life would be worth living without good friends." – **Freddie, 12**

"I'd say friends are very important. They're the only people who will offer you honest opinions about your life, whilst actually caring about what you're doing with it; this isn't really something you can get from your family, since they generally don't always see every side of your personality. Your parents also often have particular expectations that you perhaps do not necessarily agree with." – **Rich, 20**

"I value my friends more than my parents because they are more like me and easier to talk to." – **Jordy, 16**

So from Rich's mature worldly views to Jordy keeping it short and sweet, even Freddie, as young as 12, realises that his friends are very important in his life.

> Friends are extremely important to teenagers; we value them over relationships with parents and family.

As for choosing our friends, it is natural that we will graduate towards peers who have common interests and values. This is probably the most important reason why friends are so important to us; as teenagers we are subconsciously changing, searching for our self-identity and adopting values of our own. We naturally want to test these values on other people. Friends are vital to do this, as many of us develop ideas and values that we wouldn't feel comfortable sharing with our parents. Therefore, it's important that we choose friends who are likely to hold approximately the same values as us so we can feel like we fit in.

> We use friends to test our values on and try out some new ones. It's important to have friends we can look to as role models.

Sometimes this means that we pick friends whose values do not fit in with those of our parents – that we fall in with a 'bad crowd'. This is one of the hardest things for parents to accept, and it's easy to see why. Apart from worrying about what your teenagers will get up to, they have abandoned you for people with values opposing the ones you have raised them on.

Often, teenagers have 'undesirable friends' just to have some fun and test the limits of their values. I have been in this situation many times before – hanging out with the bad crowd just to have some fun – and so has Rich, so has Sam, so has Alex... lots of my friends have. We might hang out with the bad crowds for a while and be a bit silly. This could last for two weeks or two years, but by the end of it we have our solid values and these normally include very few of the values of the 'undesirables'. They may include *some* 'bad' values – like smoking, getting drunk or having dreadlocks – but as a parent these may be things you will have to compromise on; your teenagers aren't the same as you and you shouldn't expect them to be.

> Falling in with a bad crowd is often about experimenting, having some fun, and testing our values to the limit.
>
> Naturally, the more respect your teenager has for you, the more likely they are going to want to take on some of your values, thus limiting the 'damage' a bad crowd will do. See chapters 1, 2, 3, 4, 5, 6, 7, 8, 9, 10, 11, 12, 13, 14, 15, 16, 17, 19 and 20 for advice on how to get your teen to respect you.

So don't fret if your teens suddenly take to a bad crowd: as Rich goes on to explain, *"The thing about growing up is that you start making your own decisions, and as with most decisions, the opinion of your peers is important. At the same time, you don't have to agree with their opinions; you can even go the opposite way, hence a level of individuality is created".*

Now, what about if you have the opposite problem and your teens don't seem to have (m)any friends? This is generally something that occurs in younger teens, but can still be evident up to college age, and normally affects the ones who are either incredibly intelligent or at the opposite end of the scale, or are in some way different from their peers.

Surely you can remember the kids at school who didn't quite fit in and had no friends. Sometimes if there were enough clever people or not-so-clever people they would form like-minded groups and be friends within those, but there were always one or two who seemed to have very few friends.

A few weeks ago I saw a guy who was always a bit picked on at school. I last saw him at school when he was about 14, so he'd be 16 now. It was amazing. Apart from not recognising him at all, he was completely surrounded by friends, and seemed to be incredibly respected – I rather envied him.

Again, a few months ago I was invited to a party by someone from my old school. At this party was a girl who had always been a bit of an outcast, like the guy I mentioned above. And, again, she now had lots of friends, and was having a great time chatting to everyone at this party.

When I asked my friend Tom what he thought about the subject of friends in general, he said:

> "Friends might not always be there for me, but my parents and family always have been." – **Tom, 15**

So for some, making friends and fitting in comes more naturally. But for others, it may take a little longer, or it might be the new surroundings of college or sixth form that finally makes it click and throws your teen into a world of social contact.

> Everybody's time will come to fit in with a group of friends.

In the meantime, it's important that your teen feels like Tom and knows he has his family to support him when he feels lacking in help from friends. If you make sure your teen knows you are there for him, he will make friends when the time is right. If you like, you could encourage him to go to events outside of school – like sports clubs or music events – but if he is to make friends in these situations he needs to want to do it for himself.

> If your teen lacks the support of friends, reassure them you are there for them whilst they build social contacts.

Homework

○ Allow your teen to have plenty of contact with his friends, during school weeks and in holidays.

○ Let your teen bring friends home, and go to their houses.

○ If your teen seems to have few friends, let them know they still have you to turn to.

Parties

Introduction

I tell the story of my first proper teenage party, letting you in on what worked and what didn't. You can help your teenager to plan parties that run smoothly using the insight you gain from this chapter.

"Thanks everyone for such a great weekend!"

"Best nite of my lyf!!!!"

"AMAZIN ONE BOIS!!!!!"

"Awesome party jess!"

"lets do it agen 2nite guys???"

When I sign onto MSN, it's easy to spot the ones who have had a great time the previous evening. And so, a few months ago, I changed my name to inform everyone of what a great evening I had had as well:

"Ahahahha Sam fell in the pond!!!"

Oooh yup. Sam stole the 'highlight of the party' award with his spectacular fall into the pond. Well, he was sort of a bit drunk, and the pond was covered in algae so he thought it was just a path. Sam took a step, went splash, and thought what a funny path it was. He took another step, went in a bit deeper, and realised he was in the pond. Consequently, we all knew whom to blame in the morning when the sitting room stank of pond water (he'd been sleeping down there).

Now, before we go any further, I must admit that this isn't going to be a comprehensive chapter on parties – no, if you want the low-down on drugs, sex and alcohol, then turn over a few pages and submerge yourself in Sex n Drugs n Rock n Roll.

Instead, here I am going to recall the story of the very first proper teenage party I held, for my 16th birthday. Using lots of insight from myself and my friends, this should be a good guide for parents whose teens are about to venture into this area for the first time.

It was my birthday. Time for a party. A proper party – no more bouncy castles, games, or Laser Quests. No. I had graduated to proper, teenage parties. That meant lots of friends, in your garden, with alcohol and loud music. Great!

"Mum, can I have a party for my birthday? I didn't have one last year, or the year before."

"Yes, I suppose so."

"Cool."

"What do you want to do?"

"I dunno, I was just gonna get everyone round, have a BBQ, sit out in the garden, play some music. A proper party."

(Picks eyebrows) "Well, yes, don't you want a bouncy castle though? Everyone might get bored."

"MUM!!!! How old am I? I'm 16. I am NOT a baby!"

"I know, I understand that, I really do, but I just think you'll all be bored sitting around. Get a bouncy castle or something, you can all mess around on that."

"OK I seriously hope you're joking."

[Pause]

"I'm not. It would be fun to muck around on a bouncy castle."

I took that as my cue to walk out.

> Remember: treat your teenagers like adults. Let them grow up when they're ready, and don't embarrass them or lose your cool by suggesting party games.

So anyway, after a few days of conversations like that, I ignored mum's suggestions of a bouncy castle and set a date for my party that was convenient with my parents. Well, I set a date that was convenient with my friends, and hoped my parents liked it.

We chose a 'start time' of 6pm on a Saturday evening. Although this probably wasn't the best time as lots of my friends live about an hour away so they would end up going home late, I really wanted an evening party, and it worked out fine in the end with most of them getting lifts back together or staying over.

Let your teen organise their party as much as possible – this is just as good practice in organisational skills as getting their home-work in on time is.

As the date drew ever closer, I frantically began calling and texting everyone to make sure they could all still come, and finding out who needed picking up from the station at what time. I really was rather nervous about the whole thing, expecting nobody to turn up and for it to be a complete disaster.

On Saturday morning mum and I went shopping for some food and drink. We had a plan – we were going to have a BBQ – so it went pretty well and no major arguments broke out. Well, except for one: mum insisted on buying a packet of 20 cheese slices for the burgers on the BBQ. I repeatedly said that nobody would want them, and took them out of our trolley. However, when we got home and unpacked the bags, I noticed mum had sneaked them back in.

To cut the story short, I was right, and there's still a packet of 20 cheese slices in our fridge.

Take your teen food shopping with you and let them choose what they want to eat – they know what their friends like. Set a budget if you need to – again working against a budget is good practice for them.

Food for lots of hungry teenagers can be expensive, so you could ask your teenage guests to contribute £5 or a pizza.

What sort of food did we buy then? Well, I wanted to keep it as simple as possible – we stocked up on burgers, sausages and chicken drumsticks for the BBQ. We managed to get a good deal on these, as there was a mini-heat wave at the time so all the BBQ meat was on promotion. We also got lots of crisps to snack on.

Of course though, mum did her usual thing and went a bit over the top with the food. We had about three types of salads, pasta, potatoes, dips, and all sorts of fancy stuff. At the end of the party it was all the fancy stuff that was left over – nobody wants to sit down with a plate and cutlery to eat food at a party. We wanted to grab a burger off the BBQ, stick it in a roll, and stand around eating it with a bottle of beer in the other hand. Look at us, we're such cool, grown up teenagers!

> Choose food that's easy to eat at a party and doesn't require cutlery – think of it as less washing up for you.

Ah yes, beer. Shall we have a little talk about alcohol? I think that might be a good idea. Now, I knew from that very first 'mum, can I have a party?' conversation that I wanted to have alcohol at my party. In the true teen spirit, however, I didn't attempt to talk to my parents about it. Talk to my parents about alcohol? How uncomfortable! Instead, I left it until we walked past the alcohol aisle in Sainsbury's.

"Err… err, umm, mum, err, can we get some drinks then?"

"Yes, what do you want – Dr Pepper? I think we should get some Coke and Fanta as well."

"Err, yeah… can we have some, err… beer, as well?"

"Beer? You don't like beer, do you?"

"Err, umm…" (trying not to be too enthusiastic) "…yeah, every-one likes beer."

"I don't know. What would you get?"

"Err, one of those or something…" (I vaguely point at a big box of beer, trying to hide the fact that I know exactly what I'd get.)

So that is how not to have a conversation with your teenager. It was successful though, as we returned home laden with twenty 20 bottles of Budweiser. It's really rather nice. Well at least Kev thought so; he managed to drink two bottles before most of the others had even arrived.

> Allow your teenager to have alcohol at their party. Either provide it yourself so you can control the amount they have available, ask their friends to bring alcohol if they want it, or a mixture of the two. Just don't ban it completely – this gives alcohol a rebellious appeal and encourages them to drink sneakily which isn't as safe. If they are going to stagger around drunk, it's a lot safer if they do it under your watchful eye.

And so my friends arrived in their masses – I certainly didn't have to worry about people not turning up. Dad went off to the station to pick lots of people up in his car, whilst I stayed at home greeting the rest of my friends. I would have loved to have seen him pick my friends up from the station though – five girls getting into a swanky BMW with some old man (dad's words) in it. Hah!

> Offer to give lifts from the local station but set a certain time to pick everyone up and drop off or you'll be driving around all evening.

People turned up, I offered them drinks, and we sat around talking. More people turned up, and it all livened up a bit. We turned the music up. We drank more beer. More people turned up with more beer. We talked some more and drank some more. Then we all ate – well, bar the ones who had drunk too much to feel like eating. And so it continued, more or less the same. Well, at one point Sam fell in the pond, and at one point we all ran havoc on the street to go to the local shop for more beer, but unfortunately it was closed. A couple of people brought guitars and basses so we had a bit of a jam, but we couldn't really convince everyone to turn the music off and listen to us instead so that didn't quite work.

My parents were around all the time, doing the BBQ, then I think they were sitting in the kitchen talking to a couple of my friends. I know, what were they thinking? I ought to lock them away – my friends *and* my parents.

My parents never really hassled us, spoilt our fun, told us off etc. but we knew they were there looking after us so it worked quite well – we definitely didn't mind having them around. Actually, at one point, my dad ran out of the kitchen and put a plastic bottle on the table, then ran away again. I knew exactly what he was doing, so yelled "run!!!" and pegged it as far as I could – the bottle contained an Alka-Seltzer which reacted with the warm water, exploded, and shot up into the air. It's cool when my dad's a bit silly like this, because he's fun to have around, and definitely not 'an embarrassing old man' or anything similar.

> Let your teen know you will be around most of the evening, but don't keep checking up on them, telling them off, embarrassing them etc. As they get older and become used to having parties and you know you can trust them, perhaps suggest you go out for the evening or across the road to a neighbour's house to give them more freedom.

Eventually, people started leaving, with the first parents coming at around 11.30pm and the last at about 1.30am. Nobody got trains back that late – most of the people shared lifts home. People who drove themselves there stayed the night, as did the people who were catching trains the next day.

Ah yes that was a good night. We stayed up, talked, watched some DVDs, and watched Sam falling asleep on the sofa with his stinky socks in our faces. We eventually decided that sleep was a good idea at about 4.30am, and dozed off pretty quickly.

> Allow your teen to have some friends sleep over after the party. It's a lot safer for them and more convenient for their parents. Also, it takes away that feeling that everything's over, and a lot of the fun in having a party is to talk about what happened, so having some friends stay the night is a great way to do that the next day.

And that, my friends, is the story of my first 'proper' party. And I'm sure you can tell, it went remarkably well.

Homework

○ Ask your teen if they would like to have a party. It's a great way for you to get to know their friends and show you're willing to treat them like an adult.

○ Chat with your friends who also have teenagers about how they organise their teen's parties.

Sex n Drugs n Rock n Roll

Introduction

A short and sweet introduction: this chapter is going to be just what it says on the box. As always, I've saved the best 'til last.

Right then, let's start with sex. Yes, sex. I'm going to say it a few times first so you stop being all embarrassed when you see it: sex sex sex sex sex sex sex sex sex sex sex sex sex. There.

I've been trying to write this chapter for a while now, thinking of things to cover, doing research into teenage relationships; I'm not embarrassed to say that, despite my front as a hardcore teenager, I have zero experience in this area. I did manage to find a friend to ask about his girlfriend, but they had recently broken up, so I think I made it worse and brought all his emotions back up. Whoops.

So, as you can tell, I haven't been too successful with this chapter so far. Until… I had a brainwave. It was amazing. Brilliant; pure genius. Why didn't I think of it before? I never thought it was possible to create *so* much interest with *such* a simple MSN Messenger nickname.

All I did, very simply, was change my MSN Messenger nickname to 'jellyellie – I need some people who want to talk about SEX'. Within seconds, I had chat windows popping up everywhere, as the 227 people on my online contact list saw my new name.

> **John says:** sex please! :]
>
> **Matt says:** why do u want 2 talk about sex?
>
> **Kev says:** I want to talk about sex. Can we talk about sex.?
>
> **Dan says:** Why do you want people to talk about sex?
>
> **Phillip says:** I'll talk about sex. Hahaha, what a strange name!
>
> **Tom says:** Talk about waaah! Someone's horny!
>
> **Val says:** Why do you want to talk about sex? :-p

(Have you noticed they're all guys?)

And so it continued, the messages avalanching in. I'm just glad my parents weren't watching – some of the stuff people said…

Ah, what did I just say? I didn't want my parents to see? Yes, that's true. It's also why I haven't been looking forward to writing this chapter: I know that everything I write will be read by my parents, my aunties, my uncles, my grandparents and other close family friends (yes, hello!). However, I think that says it all: teenagers can have the best relationships with their parents, but some things are still off-limits in discussion, sex and drugs the two main things.

> No matter how good our relationship with you is, sex is still an incredibly awkward topic to discuss.

So undeniably, like every generation before us, there is still a big taboo and awkwardness between parents and their offspring when it comes to sex. But has anything changed, or should you assume we get up to much the same stuff that your generation did?

Well, if we look at the teenage pregnancy statistics, it's not a very pretty sight. The UK had about the same rate of teenage pregnancies in the 1970s, but whilst other European countries got these rates down over the next two decades, the UK's teenage pregnancy rate is now the highest in Europe.

Whilst I could reel off thousands of statistics about the subject, it won't add much to our discussion. Instead, there is one report that stood out to me that I would like to mention: in 1999, the Government published the *Teenage Pregnancy Report*. The report concluded that there was no single cause of the UK's exceptionally high teenage pregnancy rates, but it could see three major contributing factors:

1 **Low expectations** – some young people have such poor expectations of future job and education prospects that they see no reason not to get pregnant.

2 **Ignorance** – teenagers lack accurate knowledge of contraception, STIs, and what it really means to be a parent.

3 **Mixed messages** – one part of the world bombards teenagers with messages telling us that sex is the norm, but another part of the world – including our parents and health institutes – hushes up the subject.

You can play a significant part in helping your teenager not to fall foul of each of these issues. However, it's this third point that I think is most relevant to us, and a major part of it is the fact that teenagers do not openly talk about sex with their parents. Of course, this is the same old thing that keeps popping up, generation after generation. We all know that discussing sex and contraception with our parents is a good way of reducing promiscuous sex in teenagers; as Rich puts it:

> "Your kids are going to have sex. You will not be able to stop them. Really, the options are either lock them in their room forever, never to talk to someone of the opposite gender, or talk them through safe sex and why it's important." – **Rich, 20**

But is it true? Do we not talk to our parents about sex? Well, I never have – and only you know the answer for your situation.

> It's important to have some sort of discussion about sex and relationships with your teenagers.

Phil, who is now 21, never received 'sex advice' from his parents. It worked out OK for him, but his experience has led him to give this advice to current parents of teenagers:

> "I think parents should give their children advice about what kinds of people are out there. Some guys/girls just want to have sex, some are more "loving"... some just don't care. To be made aware of the differences in people is much more effective than talking about all the "gory" parts of sex that kids don't want to hear coming from their parents' mouths." – **Phil, 21**.

That is just one angle of approaching the age-old parents-don't-talk-to-their-kids-about-sex discussion, and I could see how it might be very successful; for starters, it's an easy way to begin a discussion about relationships. It's also a very good starting point to then move on to more serious discussions about sex and, if you dare, contraception. Finally – and perhaps most importantly – it lets us teenagers know that our parents are willing to discuss serious matters with us, aren't embarrassed about it (much), and do care for us in these ways.

As for what kind of advice you could give, Phil goes on to suggest that…

> "If parents want to help their children when it comes to relationships, then I suppose it's important to tell them to wait for the right person to have sex with, or fall in love with; especially the first time. This counts for both male and female. Guys act like they "don't care" as much as girls, but there's no reason for them to have any less emotion. So, parents need to just 'be there' really, to offer advice." – **Phil, 21**.

It's all very well me telling you how to speak to your teenagers about sex, but would I really want to speak to my parents about it? Well, it's tricky. I know that when the time comes, yes, I'll probably have to speak to them about it in some way or another – even though, as Harry says:

> "I don't really want to talk to my parents about that shit, it gets just a lil' embarrassing." – **Harry, 15**

So although we would like to avoid it for as long as possible, it might take some of the worry off our minds if we know that you guys are willing to talk to us about it.

Advice such as Phil's could start in the form of 'I once had a boyfriend who was a total pig!' which is an easy way of starting a conversation with your teenage daughter. So start off natural, chatty, and informal – never sit your teenager down for a discussion and call them into the room, as they immediately think they've done something wrong and will be nervous for the rest of the conversation.

> If you want to have a discussion with your teenagers about sex, start off informal and chatty, and go easy on the gory parts.

I think it's also important to note that even if you do think your teenager has started having sex and you are worried about what they get up to, it's never too late to have a discussion with them about it. They may feel that their relationship with you has gone beyond repair so they'll just sleep around even more; a five minute chat with you might change their mind completely.

> As the old saying goes, it's better late than never: if you think your teenagers have already started having sex, still try and have an informal chat with them about it.

So we've covered the theory: how to talk to them. But what about the practical? Is she *doing* it with her boyfriend? Under your roof?!

Quite frankly, there are no easy answers in this situation. If your teenager is 16 or over, they are doing nothing wrong in the eyes of the law; whether you want them having sex under your roof is something for you to consider personally, as every parent will have different moral views. Simply put, in this circumstance, there is one thing for you to seriously take into consideration: if you tell your teenager they are not allowed to have sex at home, it won't stop them from having sex. Their desire for lust will only be taken elsewhere, perhaps in more risky locations and with people you won't know. Instead, if you tell them you are happy to see them in a loving relationship with someone they can trust, strike a compromise: they are welcome in your home as long as you can be sure they are practising safe sex.

Oakes tells us how his mum earnt maximum respect in a similar situation:

> "I had my first serious girlfriend about a year ago. We'd been going out for quite a few months, and we hung out at my house quite a bit – my family all got on really well with her. My girlfriend and I felt that we were ready to move our relationship up a level, and I think my mum could sense what was on the cards – one day I came back from college and she had put a box of... er... condoms on my desk, with a little note. It was really cool, as I was dead embarrassed at the thought of having to buy them myself."
> – **Oakes, 17**

If you do follow this route and buy condoms or take your daughter to the doctor to go on the pill, it's important to stress that you are doing this because you want them to be safe in a loving relationship; it's not a green light to sleep around.

> It might help your teenager if you offer to buy them condoms if you know they might be considering having sex for the first time with a long term girlfriend/boyfriend. Be sure to reiterate the reasons why you are doing this.

As we close on the subject of sex, I have some final words of wisdom to leave you with: *"Remember, one parent at a time... don't double-team your kid and scare him/her from ever EVER having sex"* – *Phil* …unless, of course, that is your plan.

So now we can cross sex off the list. Phew. Got that tricky one over with – hope you're still with me. If you are, I obviously need to step it up a bit to shake you all off – OK, well let's talk about drugs! Drugs drugs drugs. Oooh such a mean looking word.

The Concise Oxford English Dictionary defines 'drug' as *"a substance with narcotic or stimulant effects".* For the purpose of this chapter, we will be looking at cigarette smoking, alcohol drinking, smoking cannabis, and perhaps touching on the general subject of Class-A drugs.

Let's start off with the lesser of the evils – in terms of legality, anyway – cigarette smoking. A document published by the NHS called *"Smoking, drinking and drug use among young people in England in 2004"* showed that girls aged 11–15 were a lot more likely to smoke than boys. The most modern survey was in 2000, when 10% of all 11–15 year old girls smoked, and 7% of all 11–15 year old boys.

The main reasons why 11–15 year olds smoke, and girls in particular, is simply a matter of trying to look cool and fitting in with a group. For this, I can be terribly lazy and direct you back to the chapter on peer pressure; remember that low self-esteem causes teens to feel that they have to fit into the group and try and be 'cool'. There are a number of ways that you can help your teenager overcome low self-esteem, including encouraging them to put themselves in new situations which they might normally be uncomfortable with, and giving them praise whenever you can.

> Peer pressure is the main reason why teenagers start smoking.

It's in this same way that young teenagers begin drinking. Drinking and smoking are seen as two of the most prominent gateways into being big grown-up teenagers, so when young teenagers abuse alcohol, it is often related to peer pressure and trying to look cool. Again the same suggestion applies for helping your young teenagers out of this rut – help them improve their self-confidence.

> When young teenagers drink it is also likely to be because of peer pressure.

For the majority of teenagers, we come across drinking in our later teenage years, when we encounter alcohol at parties and in our social groups. Some of us have friendship groups with a heavy emphasis on drinking, and others leave their teenage years without having gotten drunk once.

Alex, 16 tells me about his drinking habits:

Alex: During term-time I drink on Friday and Saturday.

jellyellie: Every week?

Alex: Most weeks. On Friday I'll buy a bottle of Buckfast (£6) and 12 cans of Druid's cider (£10). I'll drink the Buckfast and 7 or 8 cans.

jellyellie: What's Buckfast?

Alex: Tonic wine, 15.8%. My favourite drink in the whole world – if it were none alcoholic, I'd still buy it to drink. Then on Saturday I'll have 4 or 5 cans left and I'll either get another bottle of Buckfast or a naggin' of Southern Comfort (whiskey, £4).

jellyellie: So where do you get the money from?

Alex: Odd jobs and pocket money.

jellyellie: Cool. And is it pretty normal amongst your friends to drink that much?

Alex: Yeah. There's only one exception – a guy I know drinks two bottles of Buckfast and 10 or 11 cans per night, and before work sometimes he drinks three bottles of wine. He's actually a machine.

jellyellie: That's crazy.

Alex: One bottle of Buckfast has me fairly drunk like.

jellyellie: Do you worry about your health though?

Alex: No. I probably should, but I'm unable to see any direct results so it just goes over my head.

jellyellie: Yeah I think that's true for most teens really, so parents, scaring us doesn't work. What about how you get hold of drink?

Alex: I hang around with people in the year above me, or college students, so on the rare occasions when I don't get served myself, I always have someone to buy it for me.

So whilst some of you may have thought that Alex drinks an awful lot, as we can see, some of his friends drink even more – albeit they are the minority.

I could interview a hundred teenagers about their drinking habits, and each one would give me a different reply, but on the whole it's true that alcohol plays a big part in most teenagers' social lives.

> Although how much and how often varies from group to group, alcohol plays a role in the majority of teenagers' social lives.

Despite the government rolling out a proof-of-age scheme, and with retailers now refusing to sell alcohol to anyone who looks under 21 unless they have proof of age that they're 18 or over, there will always be ways for us to get our mitts on some alcohol. For some teens, it's as easy as getting their parents to buy it for them, but even this comes in different forms:

"My mum was happy to buy me some Bacardi Breezers to drink sensibly at home from when I was about 15. I guess my parents drink quite a bit – but they drink responsibly – so it's normal in my house." – **Samantha, 17**

"When dad goes shopping he always picks up some beers for me. I save them 'til my mates come round and we all get drunk." – **Scott, 15**

"I suppose my parents are pretty unusual about drinking. Whenever we go to a pub for a meal my dad always buys me a beer and tries to get me to have drinking competitions with him." – **Jed, 16**

Samantha's situation may be a good approach to take as it removes the prohibition appeal factor from drinking. As Samantha has respect for her parents and sees them enjoying alcohol sensibly, she is introduced to alcohol as a relaxing drink, not something to binge on. This could be debated in itself – is it right to encourage the regular use of alcohol as a means of relaxing? – but in general it is more positive if teenagers regard alcohol as a sensible drink rather than something to get wasted on.

> If you are happy to buy alcohol for your teenagers to drink at home, make sure you drink responsibly around your teens so they know it is not a tool for getting wasted, but a sensible, refreshing drink.

However, if this respect for their parents is missing, the teenager is likely to abuse their easy access to alcohol. As in Scott's situation, it seems that his parents might buy him alcohol to try and gain his respect, but because they haven't laid down any sort of boundaries or rules for its use, there is nothing for Scott to actually value and respect. Scott's parents might have thought they were being cool by buying him alcohol, but without boundaries for its use, teenagers just see this as a sign of our parents being weak and giving in to buying us drink.

> Make sure you set out certain rules for the usage of alcohol you buy your teens.

Jed, 16, explains what he thinks of his parents having a similar attitude:

jellyellie: Do you think it's good that your parents are encouraging you to drink?

Jed: No. I think it's f'ing irresponsible and awful.

jellyellie: Have you ever told them that?

Jed: Yep. In the form of "I *don't* want anything to drink" while at a bar on holiday.

jellyellie: And what did they say?

Jed: Response from dad: lightweight.

jellyellie: Yikes.

So for Samantha, Scott and Jed, on the surface their situations are the same: their parents are happy to buy them alcohol and encourage them to drink it. But as we have seen, there are very different factors influencing their parents' actions, and the outcomes are very different.

In short, if you are happy to buy alcohol for your teenagers and for them to drink it at home, it's important that you lay down specific rules about drinking that they must follow. Allowing them to do what they like is not what will earn you respect; on the contrary, it is setting a good example and being consistent with the rules you lay down that will make your teenagers respect you.

For other teenagers, their parents are strictly against them drinking alcohol. It's hard to say what is the right balance to strike, but at the end of the day the majority of us will drink at parties and with our friends, and I think it is something you will have to accept is just part of being a teenager. Some of us may be sensible when we drink with our friends at parties, and others will purposely set out to get as drunk as possible. In these circumstances, the most important thing is that you know where we're going to be so you can make sure we get home safely or stay with a trusted friend.

> If you know your teens are going out drinking, make sure you know where they are and if they can get home/stay the night safely.

For you to know where we are and what we're doing, we'll obviously need to have told you. And as I have mentioned before, we are only likely to tell you parents what we're up to if we know you won't be angry. Let your teens know that you would rather they tell you what they get up to than go and do it anyway without you knowing. For this to work you have to tell your teens that you won't be angry whatever they tell you, and you must then keep to your word.

This is largely the same principle that I think parents should keep in mind when dealing with their teenagers and drugs – and when we talk about drugs from now on, I mean illegal ones.

Now I know from experience that cannabis is the drug that teenagers come across most frequently, and the NHS report *"Smoking, drinking and drug use among young people in England in 2004"* agrees – in 2004, 25% of 11–15 year olds and 52% of 15 year olds had been offered cannabis, a higher percentage than any of the other most common types of drugs.

Again, this is another tricky section for me to write, because I know my parents will read it. However, as much as I'm bricking myself about letting them know what I think – I know they don't approve – I think it's important I tell you my true thoughts and feelings.

So before we go on let me tell you where I stand with cannabis, because in case you haven't sensed, I tend to be rather opinionated and liberal in my views.

And indeed, you've probably guessed correctly: I believe that cannabis should be legalised. As much as I would like to dedicate a whole chapter to the subject of why I think this, it's not really relevant. Instead I will talk about the drug from the general teenage perspective. Hopefully it will give you an insight into our thoughts, and this might help you if your teens smoke cannabis – or if you just want a good read, because I write so damn well.

Now you may find this hard to believe after what I've just said, but as much as I'd like to try it, I don't actually smoke the ole' weed as I know my parents don't approve, and I would feel terribly bad doing it behind their backs. So maybe that's a tip in itself – if your teenagers have enough respect for you they will steer clear of drugs – but I think I just have an unusually guilty conscience. In fact, the interview below confirms that it is my guilty conscience not respect for my parents that's holding me back. My friend Leon, 16, does smoke cannabis, choosing to hide it from his parents, despite having an excellent relationship with them.

> **jellyellie:** So Leon, correct me if I'm wrong, but you smoke cannabis don't you?
>
> **Leon:** Yeah. I started smoking it last summer, just gone 15. Smoked speed once as well, and taken mushies loads of times.
>
> **jellyellie:** OK, well let's concentrate on the smoking marijuana to start with, because it's probably the most common issue that parents will have with drugs.
>
> **Leon:** True.
>
> **jellyellie:** Why did you start smoking it?

> **Leon:** It gives me something to do in an otherwise utterly boring environment, and it's great craic!

As Leon's comment goes to illustrate, more often that not, boredom is the main reason why teenagers try cannabis and other more dangerous drugs. They may be perfectly intelligent, mature, high-achieving teenagers, but if boredom sets in, then anything can happen.

> Boredom is one of the most common reasons why teenagers start taking drugs. To help your teens out of this rut, support your teens in any hobbies and interests they may have.

If your teen is smoking cannabis or taking other drugs and you fear boredom might be why they have gone down this path, one tip would be to concentrate your efforts on getting them doing other activities that naturally interest them. This is a positive outlook and would be better than constantly thinking about how you can get your teens to stop taking drugs.

> **jellyellie:** Did you make a conscious decision to start smoking cannabis? Or did you just happen to be in a situation where it was offered to you, and didn't really have any views on it either way, but decided to try it?

> **Leon:** Well, I didn't wake up one day and think "I'm gonna buy a quarter today". Some lads I knew were going in on smoke so I went in on it with them. It wasn't peer pressure at all though.

Because I know how strong-willed Leon is, and how deep-set his values are, I know that he is telling the truth when he says that it wasn't peer pressure that made him take drugs.

However, peer pressure does make teenagers take drugs, just as it makes us drink and smoke. If you think this may be why your teens have started taking drugs, the same basic principles apply to combating peer pressure: raise your teenager's self-esteem and self-confidence as early as you can, giving them praise and encouraging them to put themselves in new situations as often as possible.

> **jellyellie:** Did you know about the risks and effects and stuff?
>
> **Leon:** I knew about the risks but I had jumped up expectations. For some reason I thought dope was hallucinogenic!
>
> **jellyellie:** All that scare-mongering!
>
> **Leon:** Indeed.

With comprehensive drug education in schools, and wide access to the internet, teenagers are often well aware of the risks and dangers drugs present. Instead, it might be useful for you to update your knowledge of drugs, as the sort of information now available and the way it is presented has changed so much from when you received drug awareness information.

Knowing what to look for and what to do if you suspect your teenagers are taking drugs can be life saving, only too literally, in some cases. Also, if you do ever feel like talking to your teenagers about drugs – perhaps just saying something in brief in passing – we will respect you a lot more if it seems like you know your facts. **www.thegooddrugsguide.com**, whilst aimed more at teenagers, is one of the best places to start and has links to other reliable drugs information websites.

Make sure you are up to date with your knowledge on drugs. The media isn't the best place to learn about drugs, so if you feel you might need to learn the facts, check out the website mentioned above.

jellyellie: And do your parents know you smoke?

Leon: They don't.

jellyellie: Have you purposefully kept it secret from them?

Leon: I have.

jellyellie: Why's that?

Leon: Because of the repercussions and the lectures, and the general atmosphere of disdain for me that would inevitably ensue.

jellyellie: You get on with them really well though don't you?

Leon: I do.

This is the point I was referring to earlier: the fact that even though Leon has a great relationship with his parents, he feels unable to talk to them about his cannabis use for fear of them being angry. Perhaps this is a one last reminder of the importance of letting your teenagers know that you won't ever be angry about anything they tell you. This trust is, after all, what makes a wonderful, close relationship.

Homework

○ It's important to have some sort of discussion about sex and relationships with your teenagers. Start off informal and chatty, and go easy on the gory parts.

○ If you are worried that your younger teens might be susceptible to peer pressure making them smoke and drink, talk to them about it and follow the advice in the Peer Pressure chapter.

○ If you buy alcohol for your teenagers to drink at home, make sure you drink responsibly around your teens. Also let them know of any boundaries relating to the alcohol you buy them – are they allowed to take it to parties? Can they share it with mates? Is it OK for them to get drunk?

○ Make sure your teenagers have plenty of hobbies and interests and have fun things to do with their friends so they're not likely to take drugs out of boredom.

○ Check out **www.thegooddrugsguide.com** to educate yourself about the most commonly used illegal drugs.

The End...

So, congratulations are in order. You've made it through the whole book, and are well on your way to becoming a first-class parent – that's if you've done all your homework…

But, like parenting, I realise that reading a book can be rather daunting, and you often forget what it was about a few days after you put it down. Obviously I hope this book hasn't been that crap, but nevertheless, I'm going to give you one final aid in mastering the art of parenting your unruly teenagers.

Throughout the book, you may have noticed that certain overarching points kept popping up in lots of different chapters. We could call these 'golden rules', rules that can be applied to a whole host of situations.

If you take nothing else from this book but remember these few golden rules, you will be a superstar parent. And as always, I've taken the unconventional route, and I've picked four – not three, or five – primary rules for you to remember.

Four Golden Rules You Must Remember

1 Be involved in your teenager's life. What it says on the tin:

- Talk to them.
- Help them.
- Ask them how they're feeling.
- Act genuinely interested in their life, their friends, and their hobbies.
- Make them feel loved.

2 Gain respect from your teenager. How?

- Be consistent with your punishment – if you threaten something, carry it out.
- Do cool, wacky things every now and again – remember the poo, the paper bag, the doorbell...?

3 Trust your teenager. For example:

- Treat them like adults; extend their privileges over those of younger siblings.
- Don't use sneaky software to monitor their internet usage.

4 Don't ever be angry at what your teen tells you.

They simply won't confide in you again.

Now, because I'm still a teeny weeny bit nervous about sending you back to your teenager, I'm going to give you one last bit of help...

Six Things You Must Never Say To Your Teenager

1 **"You're spoilt!"** – feel free to say this Number 1 Antagonistic Phrase to your teen if you rather fancy the idea of an hour-long argument.

2 **"Never, ever meet up with anyone you meet online."** – if you want your teens to meet up with online friends behind your back, this is exactly what you want to say.

3 **"If we catch anyone drinking at your party you'll never be allowed one again."** – by using the phrase "if we catch...", you are almost inviting your teenager to try and get away with it. And again, by banning something outright, you can be sure that if the opportunity does arise to have a drink or two, your teenager will do it anyway behind your back – even less safe.

4 **"Get a job or I'll ground you for a month."** – instead of embarrassing yourself by handing out a threat you know you won't carry out, support your teen and help them find a beneficial job they will enjoy doing.

5 **"Go to school or I'll tell the police you're truanting."** – again, instead of trying to threaten your teenager into doing something, have a chat with them and find out exactly why they aren't going to school.

6 **"Turn that bloody racket off!"** – eh, excuse me... Did you not listen to a word I said in the Music chapter? Use your interests in music as a bridge for parent-teenager communication.

And so, armed with a book of knowledge, four golden rules and six never-nevers, I'm proud to send you back to your home, back to your family, back to your teenager. It's time for you to rejoin the big bad world, and take a giant leap forwards in your relationship with your teenager. I'm sad you have to leave, but I hope it's not forever.

Maybe, just maybe, the next time I walk into a bookshop I might see you standing there, looking at my book on the shelf...

Contact us

You're welcome to contact White Ladder Press if you have any questions or comments for either us or the authors. Please use whichever of the following routes suits you.

Phone: 01803 813343

Email: enquiries@whiteladderpress.com

Fax: 01803 813928

Address: White Ladder Press, Great Ambrook, Near Ipplepen, Devon TQ12 5UL

Website: www.whiteladderpress.com

What can our website do for you?

If you want more information about any of our books, you'll find it at www.whiteladderpress.com. In particular you'll find extracts from each of our books, and reviews of those that are already published. We also run special offers on future titles if you order online before publication. And you can request a copy of our free catalogue.

Many of our books have links pages, useful addresses and so on relevant to the subject of the book. You'll also find out a bit more about us and, if you're a writer yourself, you'll find our submission guidelines for authors. So please check us out and let us know if you have any comments, questions or suggestions.

Fancy another good read?

If you've enjoyed *How Teenagers Think* how about trying a couple more of our books? If, heaven forbid, you've ever felt that your teenager could keep their room looking a bit smarter, or help out around the house somewhat more (and more willingly) than they do, you'll find *Tidy Your Room Getting your kids to do the things they hate*, by Jane Bidder, is just what you need. As PTA Magazine said, "This sensible and no-nonsense guide focuses on how to get your children to help around the house. Author Jane Bidder has filled each page, neatly bullet pointed, with top tips interspersed with examples from real-life parents."

Roni Jay's *Kids & Co Winning business tactics for every family* sets out how you can use the same techniques at home as you do at work to get your colleagues, customers and suppliers – and your children – to co-operate. It's a fun and hugely practical guide to having a great relationship with your kids. According to Woman magazine, "*Kids & Co* by Ros Jay is a clever book on how to get your kids to do what you want. The basic idea is to treat children as if they're tricky customers and use negotiating skills to win them over." And John Cleese gave the book a strong endorsement, saying, "Ros Jay has had a brilliant idea, and what is more she has executed it brilliantly. *Kids & Co* is the essential handbook for any manager about to commit the act of parenthood, and a thoroughly entertaining read for everyone else."

Here's a taster of what you'll find in *Tidy Your Room*, followed by an extract from *Kids & Co*. If you like the look of either of them and want to order a copy, you can call us on 01803 813343 or order online at **www.whiteladderpress.com**.

Extract from *Tidy Your Room*

How to get 12 to 18 year olds to do the things they hate

Jobs they can do

Here are some jobs they should be able to do.

Cleaning shoes

Give them their own shoe cleaning kit and show them how to use it. You can make one up cheaply with a shoe box and essentials inside. Or you can buy one of those sachets like moistened tissues which don't need much elbow grease. Set aside one day of the week and a time when everyone in the family cleans their shoes. Sunday night is a good one.

Definitely get them to do their own trainers. Teach them to knock them against each other (the shoes, not the kids), *outside* the house and not in, so all the dirt is outside.

Shopping

If you're worried about them going shopping on their own, or if their little hands can't cope with heavy bags, set them up on the computer and get them to do a home shop for you. Arm them with a list first so they more or less buy the right things. And always check what they've ordered before keying in your credit card details. We suggest you do the latter yourself otherwise they might just be tempted to use your card for other things.

Put it in the microwave

This is a job that any streetwise kid worth their salt should know how to perform. So next time they moan that they're hungry (even though you've just cooked them a four course meal), teach them to read the microwave instructions and press the right buttons.

Work the washing machine

And the tumble drier. Also check your guarantee in case they break it in the process. Teach them to empty the filter which is usually located at the bottom of the machine. Many an adult doesn't know how to do this until the repair man says 'Didn't you read the instruction booklet?'

Dishwasher

Don't just teach how to load it or put it on. Also explain how to put dishwasher powder in and salt.

Empty the vacuum cleaner

Preferably into the bin and not on the floor.

Move furniture to vacuum underneath

This one's for older children.

Empty your bin

Give each of them their own bin for their bedrooms. Try a different colour for each child. Make one day a week the 'bin cleaning' day. Ideally, make it the same day as your dustmen come. Then get them to put out the family bin at the same time.

Wash the bath out

Give them a pinny and make it fun. Give them the right cleaning materials and don't expect a brilliant job. But it will be a start. Next time, you can start them on the taps. Show them how to wrap a flannel round them and give them a buff.

Tidy the linen cupboard

If necessary, just get them to do one shelf. It's better than nothing.

> **Top tip**
> One friend got her kids to design shelf labels on sticky labels, for example towels, sheets etc.

Dusting

Give them a bright feather duster to make it more fun

Tidying up other people's bedrooms

Get them to sort out your own dressing table and or bedroom. Other people's rooms are always more interesting than your own. But make sure you hide any incriminating evidence first.

Give each child a 'tidy tray' or drawer

Get them to put things in it that they come across – they can do this for others in the family too. Set aside a certain time every week for putting these things back in the right place.

Use the stairs

I have a friend who has taught her children to put stray items at the bottom of the stairs. Every time someone goes up, they take something and put it away.

Under the bed

Isn't it funny how kids often love the things you hate? One of my worst jobs is crawling under the bed to vacuum, only to find things that have been left there for years. But ask the kids to clean under the bed and explain what a great opportunity it is to wriggle around in the dark, and they'll jump at it.

> **Top tip**
>
> Allow them to keep any 'finds' they come across like coins or other treasures.

Answering the telephone nicely

Even well brought up children can let you down on the phone with a 'Yes' or 'What?' when they pick up the receiver. This one can only be achieved through constant nagging and also – it has to be said – setting the right example. Try writing down an agreed phrase and getting them to repeat it, parrot fashion.

You could encourage them or give them practice by allowing them to record a message on the answer phone. But do make sure it's clear and to the point. What might seem cute to adoring parents can actually be very yuk to callers.

...and taking messages

'Someone rang,' is a favourite message via my son. Not who – he often can't even remember if it's male or female – but someone. So leave a pad of paper by the phone; preferably one that's big enough for them to see with an extra large jumbo pen or pencil firmly attached. Divide into columns with a heading for the caller, one for the time of call, another for the message, and one for the caller's phone number. With any luck, you'll get at least one of them.

Picking up their bathroom towel

Otherwise they have a wet one the next day. And no, *don't* pick it up yourself.

Clearing away old newspapers

Do this the day before the refuse collectors come. Make it a routine and they should (one day, before they leave home) do it automatically.

Cleaning out the fridge

A great way of teaching them how to spot sell-by dates. You can also use the opportunity to explain basic food rules like not storing raw meat next to cooked meat. Then, with any luck, they'll remember how not to give themselves food poisoning when they move into a student house.

Cleaning the loo

Another one that will come in handy when they have homes of their own. Someone will thank you for it one day.

Basic cooking

Teach them how to bake a potato; make an omelette; etc.

Bring down mugs from their bedrooms

If/when they don't, refuse to make them another cup of tea or coffee until they comply.

Motivation skills: generate enthusiasm in your children

Everyone is motivated by different things. But there are certain techniques you can use as a manager of either children or staff, which will help to motivate anyone. There are three key techniques:

○ Show them how they fit into the big picture
○ Set clear and realistic targets
○ Involve them

Show them how they fit into the big picture

The technique: Let your staff see how their job fits in with the whole organisation. Show them what else goes on and explain how their role meshes with it. Let them see the results of their hard work: if they make wheel bearings for the cars you manufacture, let them drive one of the finished cars.

Your child is part of the whole family, and they need to understand their place in it. You might tell them that you can't take them out on Thursday; it may be their school holiday, but you've still got to go to work. But don't just leave it at that. Explain (helpfully, without lecturing) why the whole family benefits from you working. If you can, let them come to work with you for a morning and see what you do.

Why not swop jobs with your child for a day? (You might need to modify this approach a little, especially for a small child.) Do it at a weekend when you don't have to go to work, or your boss might be a little surprised to see a smartly dressed six year old rolling up at the office and settling down on your chair, peeping up over the desk. Get your child to cook the dinner, wash the car, do the cleaning or whatever you do, while you do whatever it is they do at the weekend. You should have a pretty easy time of this (you're excused hanging around the shops pointlessly for hours with a large group of 14 year olds). Do their chores for them, though, before you put your feet up.

The object of the exercise is not to be able to say "See! I work my fingers to the bone all day while you do nothing." It is to help them see how what they do fits in (or otherwise) with what everyone else does. Make it as fun as you can. If you have more than one child, let them assume collective responsibility for all your chores, while you do all theirs.

Set clear and realistic targets

The technique: If you want people to improve their performance, you have to agree realistic targets for them to attain. If you don't, they don't know when they are doing well, which is a strong demotivator. So agree that their conversion rate of enquiries to sales should rise from 20 to 25 percent in the next three months, or that all brochures should be sent out within 24 hours of being requested.

How often have you said to your child, "You're going to have to clean the rabbit hutch out more often", or "Your bedroom's always such a mess: do something about it", or "Stop waking us up so early in the morning. Play for a bit by yourself first"?

We all do it, but we've only ourselves to blame when nothing seems to change. Of course they won't clean out the rabbit hutch more often – they haven't a clue what 'more often' means. Every day? Twice a week? And there's an added implication that you're not really bothered: if you were, you'd clarify what you want properly to make sure it really happened.

Maybe you reckon they should tidy their bedroom every Saturday morning (although the amount of garbage that can collect in a teenager's bedroom in the space of seven days might seem like more than any human could shift in a morning. And the entire family supply of mugs and teaspoons will have vanished into the gloom by Tuesday). Perhaps they should start their homework by 5.30 every evening. They could aim to clean out that rabbit hutch once a week, at the weekend, and top up the sawdust every Wednesday. And you could set an alarm for 8 o'clock for your four year old to let them know it's OK to wake you up now. (The next stage is to get them to do it by kissing you gently on the cheek instead of exploding in through the door and leaping on to the bed with a yell of "Wake up! NOW!")

Involve them

The technique: Always tell people what's going on in the organisation as far as you can. Ask for their ideas and suggestions when problems need solving. It should go without saying that you must be seen to be listening to the answers, too, even if you don't eventually act on them. Involving people makes them feel they have a stake in what's going on, so they care more about it. And when it's a success, of course you must acknowledge their part in it.

It's easy to leave our children out of what's going on, and expect them to follow on blindly. With small children this is especially true. We tend to stick them in the car without even telling them where we're going – and then get annoyed if they complain when we get there. But it's not surprising really that they resent being dragged off to places without a by your leave – how would you feel? Older children tend to ask for the information, but it still makes them feel unimportant (to you) if they had to ask.

Of course, we generally leave our children uninformed because the matter at issue is nothing to do with them, or we think they wouldn't be interested. But this is missing the point. Obviously when you tell your 12 year old that the frumpy middle-aged woman who's just turned up is going to measure your bedroom chair for a new cover, you hardly expect them to get over excited about it. But at least you've demonstrated that they have a right to know what's going on. And until you tell them, who knows what they might be thinking? Perhaps they were imagining that she was a neighbour coming to complain about the loud music coming from their bedroom, or a travel company rep come to tell you you've won a family holiday abroad, or an animal welfare officer come to take away the poor, neglected rabbit.

Suppose you have a family problem. Say your children are getting old enough to have their own rooms but you're not sure how to fit them in. Do you move house? Divide a room in two? Build an extension? Whatever you do, involve the children. Explain the problem, and ask them what they think. They may have an idea you haven't thought of: "Why not convert the garage and I'll have a bedroom downstairs?" Whether you take their advice or not, if they've been involved in the discussion, they are far more likely to be motivated to go along with whatever solution you finally reach.